THE STRUCTURE OF
WEAVING

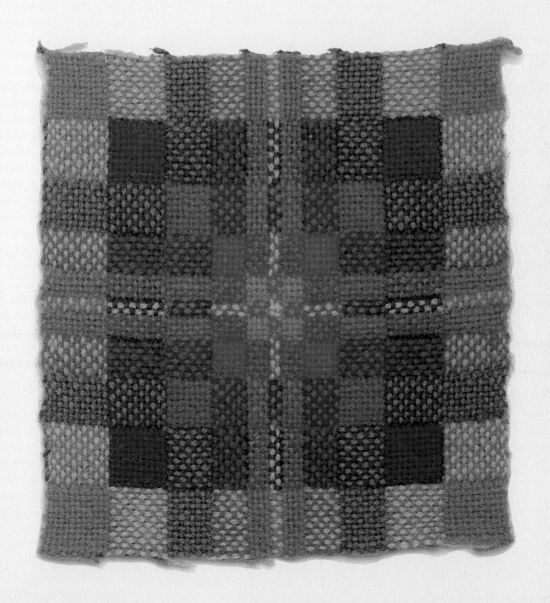

ANN SUTTON
THE STRUCTURE OF
WEAVING
PHOTOGRAPHY BY DAVID CRIPPS

Lark Books

Asheville, North Carolina, U.S.A.

CONTENTS

Lark Books
A division of Lark Communications Corp.
50 College Street
Asheville, North Carolina 28801, U.S.A.

Copyright © Ann Sutton 1982
Photographs Copyright © David Cripps 1982
Designed and produced for Lark Books by
Bellew & Higton Publishers Ltd
17-21 Conway Street London W1P 6JD England

Library of Congress Cataloging in Publication Data

Sutton, Ann.
    The structure of weaving.

    Includes index.
    1. Handweaving.   I. Title.
TT848.S89   1983   746.1'4   82-24941
ISBN 0-937274-08-9

Diagrams by Gordon Cramp Studios and Carolyn Jones

First Edition

Half title
Double cloth with padded areas. (A.S.)

Title Page
Cotton warp, mohair weft. 'Swazilace'. Designed by Coral Stephens,
and hand-woven in Swaziland for Jack Lenor Larsen, New York.
(Sample supplied by Homeworks, London)

Contents
Silk herringbone with reversals (see page 100).
Weft stripes of space-dyed yarn. (Julia Ford)

Introduction

This book is for everyone interested in woven textiles, both those who weave them and those who use them. Its purpose is not to teach how to weave (many other books do this very well) but to explain one of the most fascinating aspects of weaving: the basic structures. It shows, in the photographs, just a few of the exciting cloths which have been produced with these weaves. It shows how to read an existing cloth, and to work out how it was woven; it also shows how to design a weave; how to adapt and alter weaves, and the endless variations which are possible on the simplest structures.

Knowledge of weave structure is as important to the design of a woven textile as the structural aspects of building are to house design. Colour, texture (the furnishings) are, of course, very important, but they must come second to the structure of the fabric.

Structure is the fundamental element in weaving: good cloths are made by careful consideration of fibre, colour, texture and sett, but the underlying weave (affecting and affected by all of these elements) is the basic formation of the character of any cloth.

Most of these weave structures can be applied to rugs (often very unbalanced cloths), with very different results. The structure, however, remains the same and for ease of understanding the majority of examples are shown as cloths in a balanced sett.

The scope of this book has been restricted to structures possible on a maximum of 8 shafts. Most of the cloths have been woven on 4 shafts or fewer. This restriction not only makes the book more useful to the average weaver, but also demonstrates that fascinating textiles do not depend on elaborate equipment or a multiplicity of shafts. It is a convenient limit within which to work, with plenty of possibilities, even in the simple 2-shaft plain weave (which forms the longest section in the book).

It is recommended that the section on reading and working out drafts should be given plenty of attention at the beginning, until it is thoroughly understood. Then the rest of the book will be easy to understand, and an extra dimension added to present skills in weaving. There are very few 'recipes' – partly because the cloths shown are the creation of their weavers, but also because the book's aim is to encourage intelligent understanding and a personal approach to design. Design in weaving does not mean the ability to draw and paint, but to observe, appreciate, analyse, question, and to be able to manipulate weaves on point-paper, in order to achieve the desired results. An important feature of this book is its colour photographs. The joy of a woven textile depends to a very large extent on its colour.

This is the first book on weaving to show **all** the examples 'life-size', which will enable the reader to understand a cloth as clearly as is ever possible from the printed page. Also with this in mind, as many selvedges as possible have been shown – these often give vital clues to the structure. All cloths have, of course, been shown with the warp running vertically. In two cases, in the section on double-cloth, the reader is able to examine the **reverse** of the cloth, simply by turning the page.

The fabrics fall mainly into four categories:

(a) historic and/or ethnic pieces interesting for their structure and full of inspiration for cloths today.
(b) cloths from a few commercial firms: Bute Fabrics (Scotland), Jack Lenor Larsen (USA) and Placide Joliet (France), whose policies are based firmly in the hand-weaving tradition.
(c) work by students, or past students, of some of the many excellent woven-textile departments in colleges of art and polytechnics throughout Britain. The work in this category is identified by the name of the student as well as the name of the college where the work was done (for example, Jessica Cox, West Surrey College of Art). Many of these students have now graduated and are professional designers/craftsmen.
(d) work by professional craftsmen and/or designers.

My very grateful thanks to everyone who lent me textiles for inclusion in this book and special thanks to the lecturers in charge of weave departments, who gave me such freedom to examine their records and samples, and helped me in every way: David Currie (Glasgow School of Art); Margaret Bide, Ann Dolley and the staff at West Surrey College of Art; Rosemary House (Central School of Art and Design); Howard Carter (Loughborough College of Art); Neville Van Hove (Manchester Polytechnic) and Jenny Hoon (Derby Lonsdale College). Also: Mike Halsey; Pat Holtom for valuable general support and some special last minute samples; John Hinchcliffe; Peter Collingwood for constructive criticism; Sue Lawrance of Homeworks for samples of Jack Lenor Larsen and Placide Joliet cloths; Peter Simpson for Bute Fabrics samples.

I have picked the brains of many weavers through their books, and gratefully acknowledge the help of Anni Albers, Hilary Chetwynd, Watson, Oelsner, Ashenhurst **et al**. (See Booklist on page 191.) Finally, grateful thanks to David Cripps for agreeing to photograph the examples for this book. He is renowned for his sensitive photography of hand-made objects, and was an obvious choice for a book to do with the examination of weaving. His photographs, as always, give that same thrill as can be experienced when handling the real thing. It was a pleasure to work with him, with his genuine interest in and appreciation of the fabrics, and he has made a great contribution towards the general design and quality of the book with his inimitable photography.

8

Balance and Sett

Balance

Balance is the relationship between the setts (see page 10) of warp and weft. The same sett, with the same yarn in warp and weft produces a **balanced** cloth. When the setts are unbalanced the behaviour of the cloth and often its colour are affected.

A **warp-face** cloth has the balance altered so that the warp is set very closely – it will often obscure the weft completely. The same yarn may still be used for both warp and weft, but the balance altered so that, for example, the warp is set at 30 epi (ends per inch / 2.5 cm) and the weft at only 10 ppi (picks per inch / 2.5 cm). This will affect both the look and performance of the cloth. For example, any stripes in the warp will become more intense in colour, and the cloth will hang well in clothes or drapery.

When the reverse is applied, the cloth is known as **weft-face** – the warp is often completely concealed by the weft, which packs down into the spaces between the widely spaced warp. This type of sett is used for most flat-weave rugs and pictorial tapestries, as it enables solid colour areas to be inserted in a hard-wearing cloth made heavy by the amount of weft yarn which it is possible to insert. Sometimes areas of both warp and weft face are used in the same cloth.

This alteration of sett and balance can, of course, be applied to any weave structure. For clarity, most of the weaves described, and shown, in this book are in a balanced, or near-balanced, cloth.

These three cloths were woven with a red warp and a green weft. The top sample is **balanced**, with the same number of warp and weft threads to the inch (2.5 cm); the middle one is **warp-faced**, with more warp threads than weft to the inch (2.5 cm); the bottom sample is **weft-faced**: the warp widely spaced so that the weft is allowed to predominate. The same yarns and weave were used in all three samples.

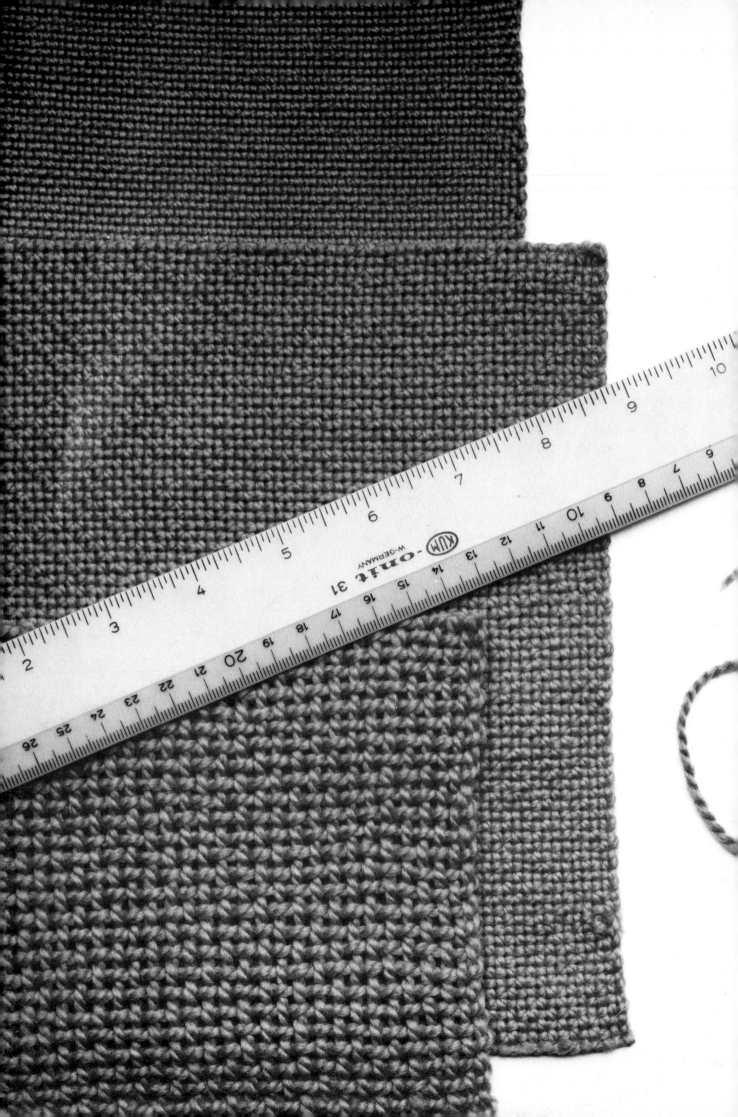

Sett

Sett is the number of threads per inch (2.5 cm) in the warp and weft. The word sett is often used to refer to the warp only, and the cloth may be described, for example, as being set at 14 epi. Metric settings are usually measured over 10 cm. The sett is extremely important to any woven cloth. Omitting or adding only one or two threads per inch (2.5 cm) can make the cloth richer or poorer, and affect the performance and handle of the cloth.

When working out the sett for a particular yarn and cloth, the proposed weave structure must always be considered in the calculations. The more intersections of warp and weft, the more open the sett should be, and vice versa. For example, if the same yarn is used for both warp and weft in plain weave (the weave with the most intersections), in theory the weft will need a space of its own diameter in order to pass between each adjacent warp thread. If the same yarn was planned in a 2/2 twill cloth, the warp could be set more closely, as the intersections of weft and warp are fewer (one intersection after every two warp ends instead of after every one as in plain weave).

These cloths were woven in balanced plain weave from the same yarn, but with different setts. The top one, set at 12 epi, is firm and hard-wearing. The middle one, set at 8 epi, is more flexible. The bottom one, set at 4 epi, makes an open cloth.

The sett is determined by winding the yarn around a ruler over 1 inch (2.5 cm) so that the threads touch, then taking a percentage of that number, depending on the weave to be used. A plain weave is sett at 50 per cent of the original number to make an 'average' sett cloth such as the centre sample.

Simple Drafting

Drafting is the process of putting a weave pattern down on paper. It is a useful language to acquire, as once mastered it can give the weaver access to all books, of whatever period, on weaving. At first, there appear to be many drafting systems – every book seems to use different symbols. However, the basic information is always the same, and once you have understood it, it is simple to adapt to the system being used.

Understanding drafting has other great benefits. It makes it possible to work out weaves which do not appear in books. It becomes easy to analyse the weave of any textile, and to work out how it was threaded, and the order of lifting the shafts. It is also possible, and simple, to design original weaves, working out how to weave them on the equipment available. Many variations can be planned, using only pencil and paper, before the warps are made, saving expensive mistakes even at sampling stage.

Point-paper

The paper used for working out weaves is called point-paper. It may be ordinary graph-paper or it may be printed specially for the purpose. It is advisable to choose a paper with not too small a square. When beginning, a 2 mm square is the minimum size on which to work comfortably. Too large a square can also be tedious to work on. The ideal size is ⅛ inch, difficult to buy as graph paper but now available for weavers in pads, with a gummed back for the convenience of fastening drafts to record cards. It also has a heavier ruling after every four squares, which is useful for working out most weaves.

Starting to draft

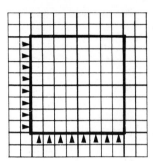

Fig. 1

When using point-paper the first thing to realise is that the spaces **between** the printed lines represent the threads (see Fig. 1).

This never varies no matter how thick, or how thin, how closely set, or how far apart, how smooth, or how textured a thread. Fig. 2 shows a set of weft threads crossing a set of warp threads. However, this does not show how they interlace to form a woven cloth. Where one thread crosses another, it must pass either above or below another thread. All weaves are composed of these two actions. On point-paper only the thread which is uppermost at this point is shown. So a draft for plain-weave looks like Fig. 3.

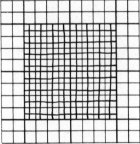

Fig. 2   Fig. 3

At this stage it is useful to begin to look at repeats of the weave or the pattern. Throughout the book, one pattern repeat will be outlined. Often, if the repeat is small, it will be repeated several times so that the joining of the repeats may be seen clearly. When working with a draft to find out how to thread and lift the shafts for a particular design, it is only necessary to copy down one repeat of the design. When several repeats are put down, they must always be shown in complete numbers, warpways and weftways. The plain weave repeat has been outlined at the bottom left corner of Fig. 3.

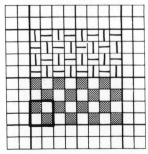

Fig. 4

Throughout the rest of the book, the more usual way of showing drafts has been adopted – that of presenting the weave in solid black and white squares. Every black square represents warp passing over weft, and every white square represents weft over warp as the plain weave draft in Fig. 4 shows.

When designing on point-paper, it is much easier, especially when a beginner, to work in the vertical and horizontal line method, as this makes it easy to see the weave. This method will therefore be used in this chapter. It will be easy to convert one method to another when using weave structures from the rest of the book. The more a weaver is able to manipulate weaves on point-paper, the greater the chance of producing interesting cloth structures.

Repeats

In the many drafts of weaves shown throughout the book one repeat of the design has been heavily outlined (usually bottom left-hand corner of the weave plan). It is customary when showing small-scale structures, to show the weave repeat four times (twice in each direction).

Abbreviations

When instructions for threading or lifting contain many repeated combinations, these can be abbreviated on paper by putting a bracket alongside the group and indicating how many times this must be repeated.

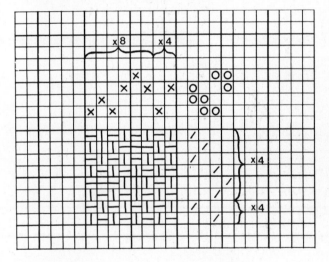

A woven dress fabric and its draft. The size of the draft is never the same as the weave in the fabric, unless the threads of the cloth are the same size as the spaces on the graph paper.

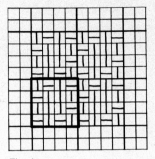

Fig. 1

Fig. 2

It is now possible to alter the plain weave slightly, extending some threads so that one thread stays on the surface for a longer distance: over three threads, instead of over one, for example. (See Fig. 1.) It is easy to imagine that this small alteration would produce little vertical marks in the cloth, in warp stripes. (Note that the repeat has now grown in size with the slightly more elaborate pattern.)

Fig. 2 shows another variation on this move.

The same extension of a couple of the plain weave threads over three instead of one has been turned alternately to affect warp and weft, producing a new all-over pattern. (The repeat is now 8 threads in each direction.)

This is the basis of weave design. In subsequent sections of the book the original 'families' of weaves (plain, twills, satin, cords, honeycombs, etc.) covered are all combinations of single units of warp-over-weft ⊡ or ▨ or weft-over-warp ⊟ or ☐

Left: plain weave. Centre: cloth woven from the draft at Fig. 1 in which some warp threads float in threes. Right: cloth woven from the draft at Fig. 2, in which both warp and weft threads float in threes.

Having plotted out the interlacing of threads (the **weave plan**) the next step is to find out how to weave it. The order of threading and the lifting sequence can both be worked out on point-paper before the warp is made.

Taking a simple **weave plan**, leave space above it on the point-paper, and also to the right (Fig. 1).

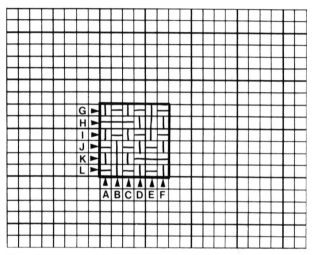

Fig. 1

To discover how to thread this particular design:
1. Look at the first vertical row on the bottom left of the weave plan (row A) in Fig. 2, and place a cross in the square above it level with the number 1.

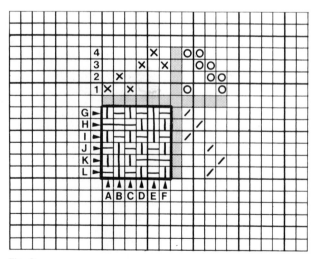

Fig. 2

It is usual, for clarity, to leave a blank row above and to right of the weave plan. (These rows are shaded in this diagram only.)
2. Look at the next vertical row B and compare it with row A. If it is a different combination of marks (which it is), place its cross on a different level (2) but immediately above the vertical row in question.
3. Look at vertical row C, and check it against A and B. It will be seen that it is exactly the same as vertical row A, so the cross must be put on the same level as that for A, but above vertical row C.

Continue working across vertical rows D, E and F, checking each one in turn against all the previous vertical rows previously worked. It will be found that vertical row F is identical with vertical row D.

The X marks now placed represent the way in which the threads must be **entered** or threaded onto the shafts 1, 2, 3 and 4 in order to weave this pattern. This procedure of finding out the threading is the same no matter how simple or complicated the design, and once understood it can be applied to all weaves. In subsequent sections of this book, the threading and lifting plans for a weave have often not been included. However they can always be worked out by copying down one repeat of the pattern and applying the method outlined above.

Having worked out the order of threading for the pattern, the next, and essential, step is to find out how to lift the shafts to weave the required pattern. Look at Fig. 2, but now at the horizontal rows in turn. Starting with the top row G, place a mark in the blank row to the right, opposite G row. (It may be helpful at this stage to cover up the other horizontal rows, H – L, with a piece of paper.) Reading across it, from left to right, look for vertical marks (indicating that a warp thread needs to be lifted at that point). The first square to the left contains a vertical mark. Follow that row upwards until stopped by an X, then track over to the right until the first of the blank rows is reached, and put an O there. Continue this process for every vertical (warp up) mark in row G. (There is no need to mark the one on C, as it is the same as A.) O marks will occur on levels 1 and 4. These are the shafts which will need to be lifted in order to weave the first row. Check row H, and the O marks lie on levels 3 and 4. It will be seen that row I is identical to row G, and so indicate that the same shafts should be lifted by placing the / mark on the same line. Rows J and L are similarly identical.

The weave plan (I–), threading draft (X), tie-up for a foot-loom (O), and order of pedalling (/) are now complete, and this fabric can be set up on the loom and woven.

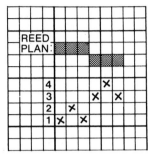

Fig. 3

Sometimes special instructions are necessary for the grouping together of certain warp threads in the reed. The design illustrated, for example, is enhanced by entering the first three ends in a dent, and the second trio in the next dent. This would be shown in a reed plan (Fig. 3), usually above the threading.

If an indication of placing of coloured or textured yarns is needed, symbols can be put by the side and base of the weave plan and a key provided. Fig. 4 shows the finished draft with all information except sett.

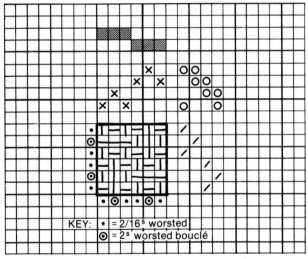

Fig. 4

Sometimes books do not provide a weave plan, but only the threading and lifting instructions. However, a weave plan can be constructed by following the above instructions in reverse. When beginning, this is a very good exercise to do, and it is rewarding to see the weave develop.

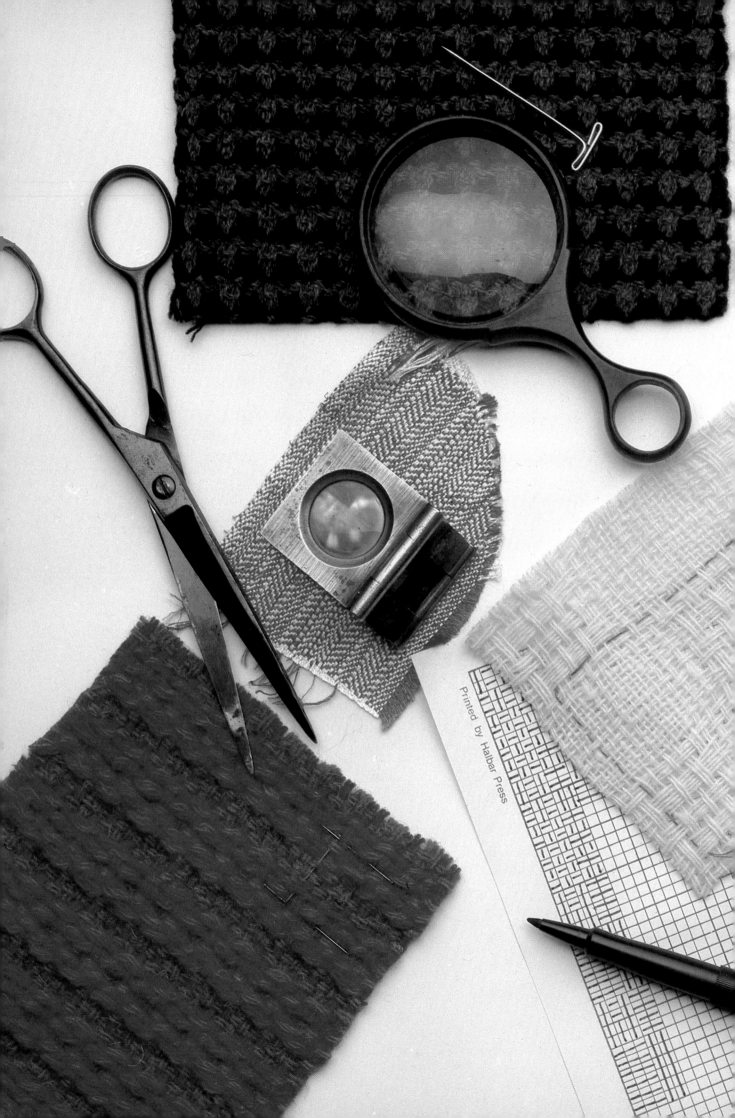

Printed by Halbar Press

Reading a piece of cloth

Using the system just described, it is possible to plot down a weave from a cloth sample and to work out how to weave it. If possible, isolate one repeat of the weave – ideally by cutting it out with scissors along the threads. The weave may also be isolated by running a thread around it with a needle, or by inserting pins in the repeat boundaries. Then read off each thread in turn (warp or weft) with the help of a pin to separate the threads, and mark the 'over one, under three, over two', etc. down on point-paper. It is often easier to have an assistant at this stage, as it is easy to lose the place in the weave when turning to the point-paper. When the weave plan is complete, the threading and lifting can be worked out in the usual way.

It is a good idea, when looking at pieces of weaving, to get into the habit of holding them up in the same position as they would be on the loom, that is, with the warp running from top to bottom. All weaving should be shown this way (except tapestry, which is often woven with the image sideways). When preparing pieces of cloth for analysis look out for clues which indicate which is warp and which is weft. Sometimes it can be very difficult to tell if no selvedge is apparent, but if the cloth is part of a garment then the cloth will usually have been cut with the warp running vertically up the garment.

It will help beginners to understand the drafts in subsequent sections of this book if the solid squares are translated into vertical and horizontal lines. These sections explore the various ways of developing new weaves and, although the traditional structures will always be interesting and used widely in many contexts, it is fascinating, and convenient, to be able to draft on point-paper exactly what the required weave should be, and work out how to weave it. Sometimes, of course, the number of shafts necessary will be more than those available. However, after only a short experience of drafting, it becomes possible to adjust drafts to enable fewer shafts to be used. A more convenient (i.e. simpler, so that fewer mistakes are made during threading) threading order may also be possible by using an **extra** shaft or two, if available. Once drafting is understood and practised, the weaver is freed from following 'recipes' and is able to create totally new fabric structures.

Various ways of outlining a repeat and of examining a weave. Often a magnifying glass will give enough magnification but a 'count-glass' will be useful for reading finer fabrics. Magenta/orange/brown cloth (Janet Taylor, West Surrey College of Art and Design) White wool cloth. (Aries, designed by Peter Simpson, R.D.I., Bute Fabrics Ltd)

Plain Weave

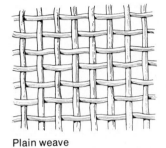

Plain weave

Plain weave, sometimes called 'tabby' by hand-weavers, is the name given to the simplest and most common of weaves. In plain weave each weft thread passes over and under successive warp threads, in opposite order to the one preceding it.

The word 'plain' indicates simplicity, and must not be thought of as synonymous with 'dull'. The variations which are possible on this structure make it the one most used in textile-making throughout the world by all cultures and in all ages. Plain weave can be woven on any type of loom, no matter how simple or primitive. It is the strongest weave, having more thread intersections than any other. Plain weave needs only 2 shafts on the loom, but in practice, especially when fine yarns are being used, 4 shafts are used to reduce friction on the threads and overcrowding of heddles. The many elements which can be varied to produce endlessly different cloths in plain weave can also apply to other weaves. The simplest variation is that of thread thickness. Without deviating from a balanced cloth (and without the help of colour, thread groupings, textured yarns or varied tension), subtle and beautiful cloths of many weights can be woven. Plain weave is often the best way to use a very special yarn, as the structure enables the threads to be set more openly than in any other weave.

Plain weave is, paradoxically, one of the most difficult of all fabrics to weave well by hand, as it needs to be sett carefully, beamed with perfect tension and woven with a constant beat.

6

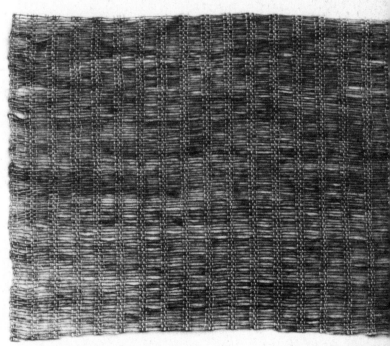

Plain weave fabrics in different fibres, balances and setts.
1. Lightweight cotton with silk check including random ikat. (Anne Vassallo, West Surrey College of Art and Design)
2. Ixtle fibre floor-cloth with selvedges on all four sides. (Mexico)
3. Thick, linen warp stripe. (Finland)
4. Brushed mohair and wool tops cloth. (A.S.)
5. All wool, balanced. (A.S.)
6. White linen spaced warp, grey linen weft. (A.S.)

1

2

3

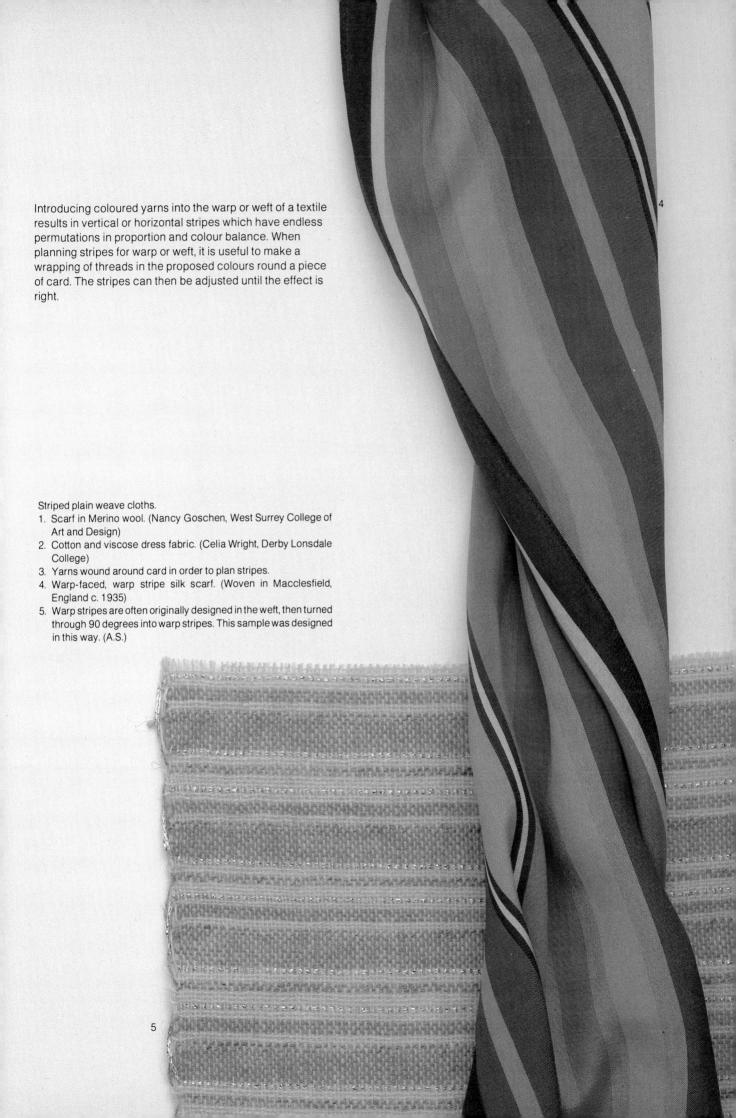

Introducing coloured yarns into the warp or weft of a textile results in vertical or horizontal stripes which have endless permutations in proportion and colour balance. When planning stripes for warp or weft, it is useful to make a wrapping of threads in the proposed colours round a piece of card. The stripes can then be adjusted until the effect is right.

Striped plain weave cloths.
1. Scarf in Merino wool. (Nancy Goschen, West Surrey College of Art and Design)
2. Cotton and viscose dress fabric. (Celia Wright, Derby Lonsdale College)
3. Yarns wound around card in order to plan stripes.
4. Warp-faced, warp stripe silk scarf. (Woven in Macclesfield, England c. 1935)
5. Warp stripes are often originally designed in the weft, then turned through 90 degrees into warp stripes. This sample was designed in this way. (A.S.)

1

2

Stripes of textured yarns, with or without a change of colour, can give very definite vertical or horizontal emphasis to a plain weave cloth. Some textured yarns, if slippery enough, like looped mohair, or smoothly textured and firmly spun, can be used in the warp without giving trouble during weaving. In order to weave some fabrics, such as those woven by the French firm of Rodier in the 1930s, it is likely that some dents were enlarged by removing wires from the reed to allow for the irregularities of the slub yarn.

Three cloths hand-woven by the French firm of Rodier in the 1930s. (Cloths lent by John Hinchcliffe)

1. Fine wool/angora with weft bands of hand-spun coarse wool slub, dyed bright yellow and orange in the fleece.
2. Natural brown wool ground with hand-spun weft stripe pulled up into loops at regular intervals.
3. Fine wool crêpe with warp stripes of hand-spun wool slub (lying over three picks and under one).

3

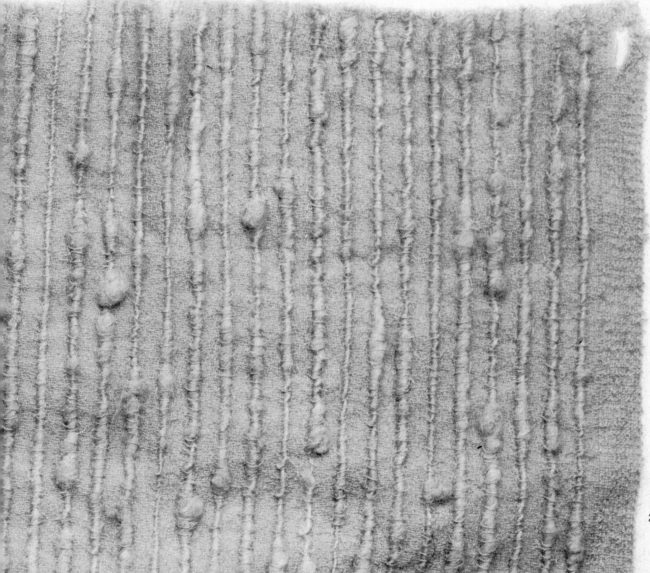

1

28

2

Elizabeth Peacock
1. Spindle-spun Nigeri...
2. Warp 2-ply Indian h...
   Indian. Warp & weft...
3. Spindle-spun Nigeri...
   " " "
4. " "
5. " "
Brown crea...
Blue
green
Greenish...
... Perl...

Crossing warp stripes with weft stripes produces checks. These can be simple and regular, such as traditional gingham, or very elaborate like tartan. Thin stripes on a plain or checked background give a tartan-like appearance; broad stripes are common in large-scale items like travel rugs. There is a convention when weaving checks for dress fabrics to weave a few more picks than ends into a check, to give an elongated 'square' which is thought to be more flattering when worn. Checks are often designed by winding stripes round a card in two directions, leaving slight gaps between the threads so that both sets can be seen.

Plain weave fabrics with coloured checks.
1. Welsh wool check. (Bridget Bailey, West Surrey College of Art and Design)
2. Yarn wrapping on card – a method of designing a check.
3. Blue-and-black check on white spindle-spun Nigerian cotton. (Woven c. 1936 by Elizabeth Peacock, Sussex, England and lent by West Surrey College of Art and Design)
4. Cotton gingham.

Overleaf:
Plain weave cloths with textured yarns forming a check design.
1. Crêpe-spun cotton ground with slub cotton check.(India, lent by Frances Hinchcliffe)
2. Two thicknesses of jute singles in warp and weft. (A.S.)

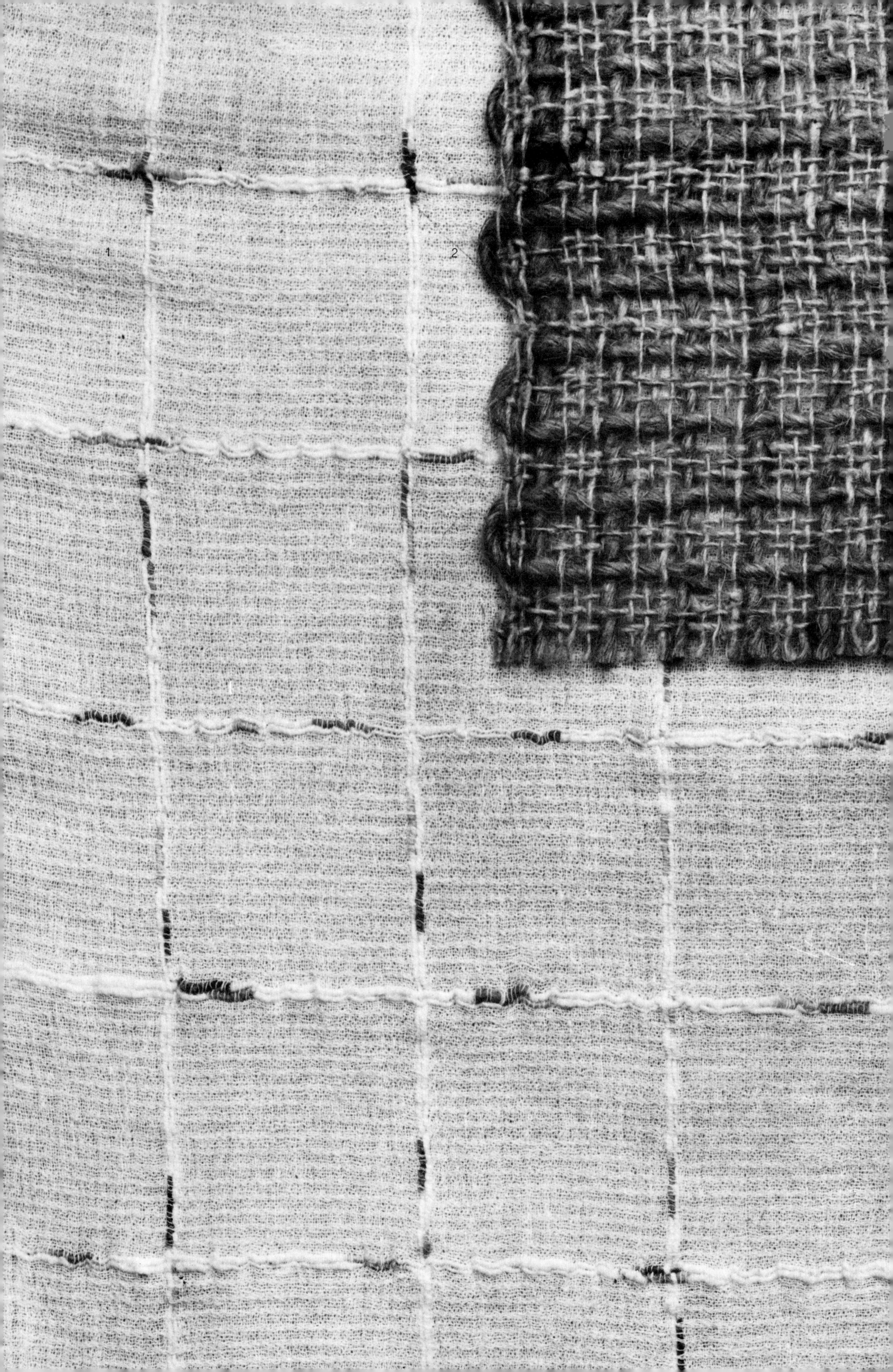
1
2

In some cloths emphasis can be given to either the warp yarns or the weft yarns. Either of these may be set so closely that the other sett of threads does not play a visible part in the cloth at all, but serves only to hold the close-sett yarns together. There is often a big difference between the thickness of warp and weft yarns, and this, together with the sett and the beat used, will affect the performance as well as the look of the cloth.

1

1. & 2. Translucent fabrics with gimp or slub cotton yarns in the warp and nearly invisible fine nylon monofilament weft.
3. Fine sewing cotton warp with hand-spun mohair weft. ('Swazi-drapery', designed by Coral Stephens and hand-woven in Swaziland for Jack Lenor Larsen, New York. Sample lent by Homeworks, London)

1

2

When alternating thick and thin yarns are used in the warp and weft with plain weave, it is possible to weave chequerboard squares. The squares 'change step' by a deliberate mistake: putting two thin threads side by side in warp or weft. The same ordering, but with colour change instead of thickness, produces an extraordinary colour-and-weave phenomenon (see page 38) called 'log cabin'.

1. Vertical stripes are formed in a plain weave based structure by alternating the colours and textures of the picks. (A.S.)
2. Plain weave with double threads (making a thick yarn) alternating with single threads. Although these also change in colour in this example, the chequerboard effect would still be visible if thick and thin threads of one colour had been used throughout. (A.S.)

Overleaf:
A typical gamp woven to illustrate some of the colour-and-weave patterns formed by the order of colouring in warp and weft. (This is a plain weave sampler.) From the left, the warp bands are: (a) all light; (b) one dark, one light; (c) two dark, one light; (d) two dark, two light; (e) one dark, three light. The sample was woven in bands of light and dark picks in the same colour combinations. (Julie Parry, West Surrey College of Art and Design)

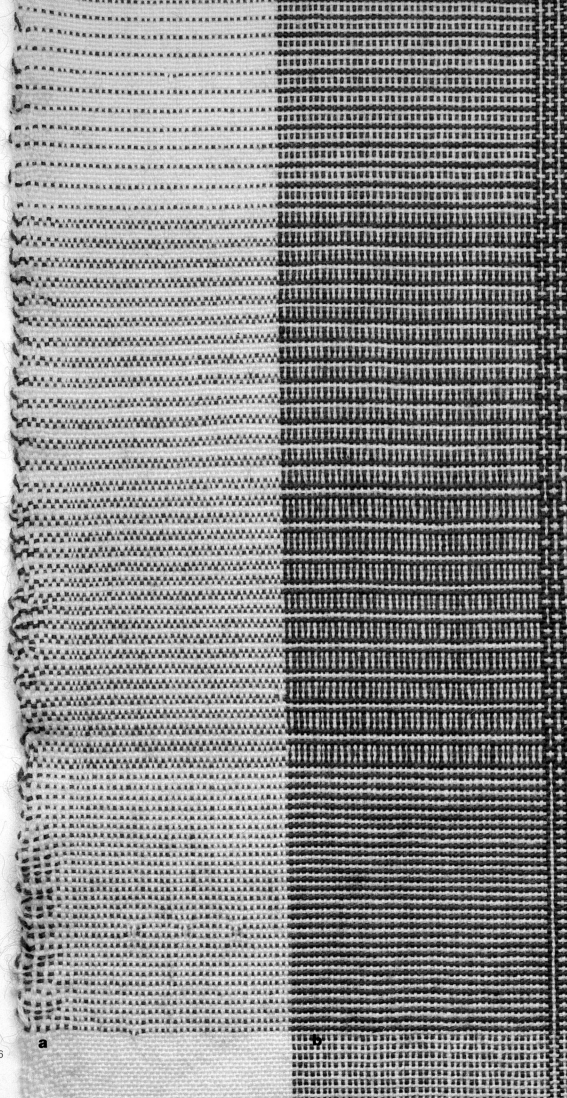

a   b   c

d

e

Colour-and-weave

Although the prime aim of this book is an understanding of structure, the part played by colour in relation to some structures is too great to ignore. This is especially so in a group of patterns known as 'colour-and-weave' because they are produced by the direct relationship of colour organization in warp and weft, and a simple weave. These patterns are familiar, usually on a small-scale, on tweeds and suitings, and unlike most patterns in woven fabrics they do not depend on the use of many shafts for complexity. Colour-and-weave designs are often based on plain weave, or on 2/2 twill. (Once the design principle is understood for plain weave, the application to 2/2 twill and other simple weaves will be obvious.)

One of the best ways to understand 'colour-and-weave' effects is to thread up a **gamp** or **blanket** of bands of warp showing different colour combinations, weaving the same combinations across, followed by any combinations of your choice. For this first sample, only two colours will be needed in the warp. Often black and white are used, or two other colours with distinct tonal contrast. Two-inch (5 cm)-wide bands of each black and white combination should be wide enough to see the resulting pattern. Some weavers like to separate the bands by a narrow warp stripe in a contrasting colour.

Bands could be composed of:
      1 black, 1 white
      2 black, 1 white
      1 black, 2 white
      2 black, 2 white
      3 black, 1 white
      3 black, 2 white
      1 black, 3 white
      2 black, 3 white
and so on.

For the sample, combinations should be woven in the same order (separating the bands by a contrasting colour if this has been used in the warp) weaving each sample for 2 inches (5 cm). Other combinations can then be tried. Unexpected little patterns occur and sometimes the most satisfactory are those where the combination crosses its own band, but often a good design will be the result of a 'sport' on another band. This is the reason for weaving a gamp or blanket.

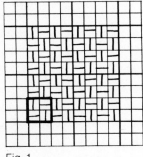

Fig. 1

It is not essential actually to weave these combinations in order to see the resulting patterns. They can be indicated on point-paper by working in two stages: First, the weave (in this case plain) is plotted lightly over an area (Fig. 1).

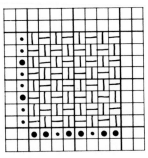

A combination of black and white threads is then indicated along the bottom, for the warp, and down the side, for the weft (Fig. 2).

Fig. 2

By using a thin felt pen, the black threads can be strengthened where they lie on the surface and appear as vertical marks in the warp (Fig. 3). Ignore the white threads.

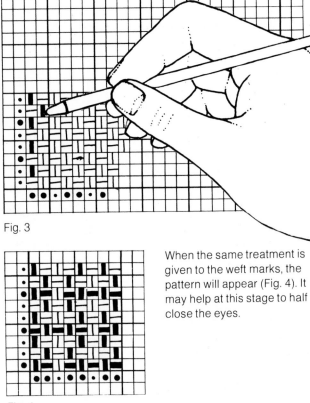

Fig. 3

When the same treatment is given to the weft marks, the pattern will appear (Fig. 4). It may help at this stage to half close the eyes.

Fig. 4

Several different colour-and-weave patterns can be woven side by side. The traditional Prince of Wales and Glen Urquhart checks are examples of cloths composed in this way based on a 2/2 twill weave. Using more than two colours will enlarge the possibilities of producing patterns from the simplest of weave structures.

Striped borders making interesting colour-and-weave patterns where they cross. Half-bleached and indigo-dyed linen. (Imogen Moffat, West Surrey College of Art and Design)

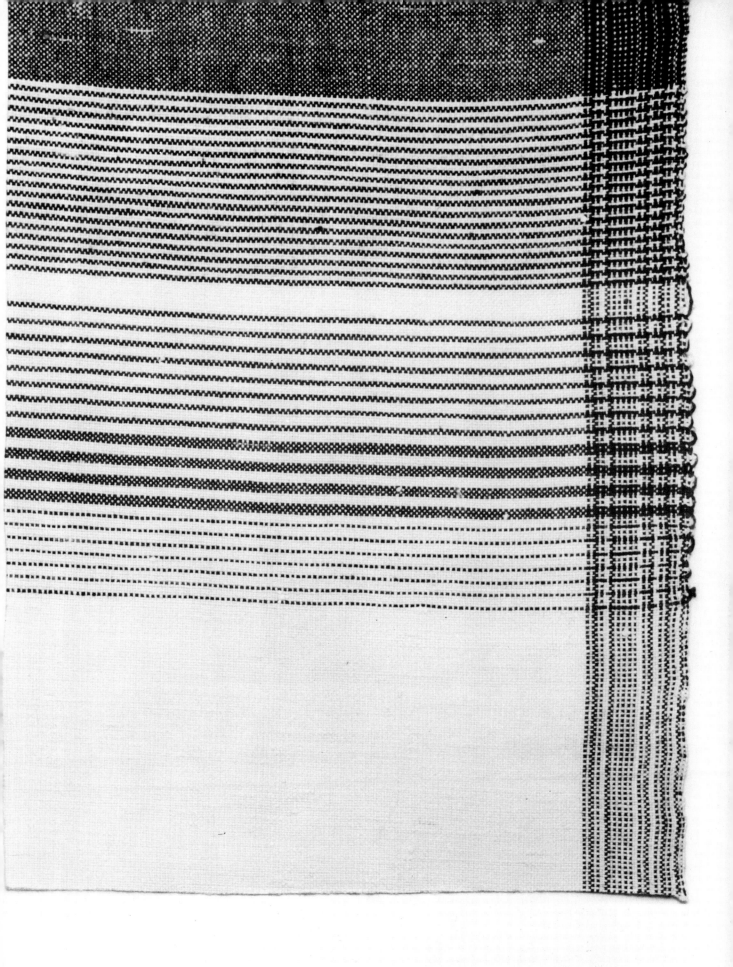

Planning a colour-and-weave motif

It is not necessary just to accept what happens in colour-and-weave. It is possible to decide what simple pattern is required and then, by adjusting the weave and colour order if necessary, to work out how to weave it. For instance, if a motif of a square-within-a-square is required, on a plain ground, plot this out on to point-paper as faintly shaded areas (Fig. 1).

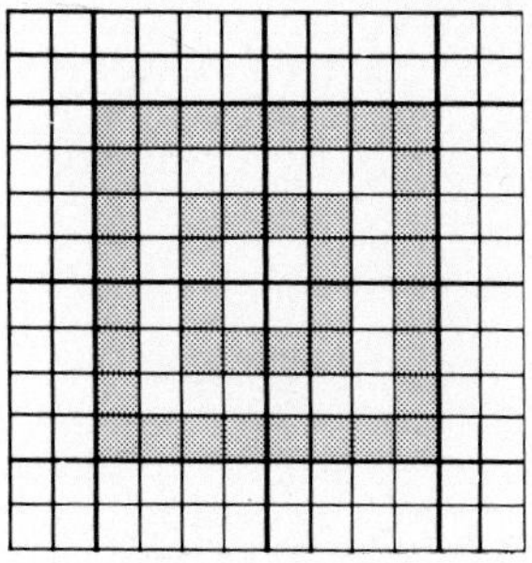

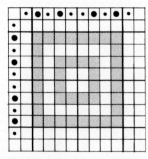

Fig. 1

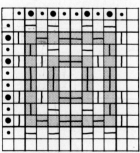

Fig. 2

The next step is to mark the ends and picks as light or dark, depending on whether the **majority** of that horizontal or vertical row is light or dark (Fig. 2).

Then the weave can be introduced. Examine every square to see whether it must end up as a light or dark area in the finished result, and whether warp or weft **must** be uppermost at that point. (Some decisions can be postponed at this stage: for example, where a dark result is needed, and both end and pick are dark, it is immaterial which is uppermost.) In other words, track each light warp end down: where it meets a dark area, the dark weft must be uppermost in that square; where it crosses a dark pick, and needs to show as light, it must be on top. Repeat for the dark ends and for the light and dark picks (Fig. 3).

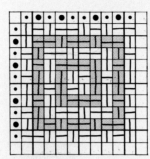

Fig. 3

The rest of the weave can now be filled in (Fig. 4). (Do this as closely as possible to a plain weave structure so that the cloth is stable and the motif clearly visible.) The threading and lifting can then be worked out in the usual way. Some adjustment may be necessary to the weave at this stage, to make it fit the shafts available.

Fig. 4

Colour-and-weave design based on squares-within-squares. (Pat Holtom)

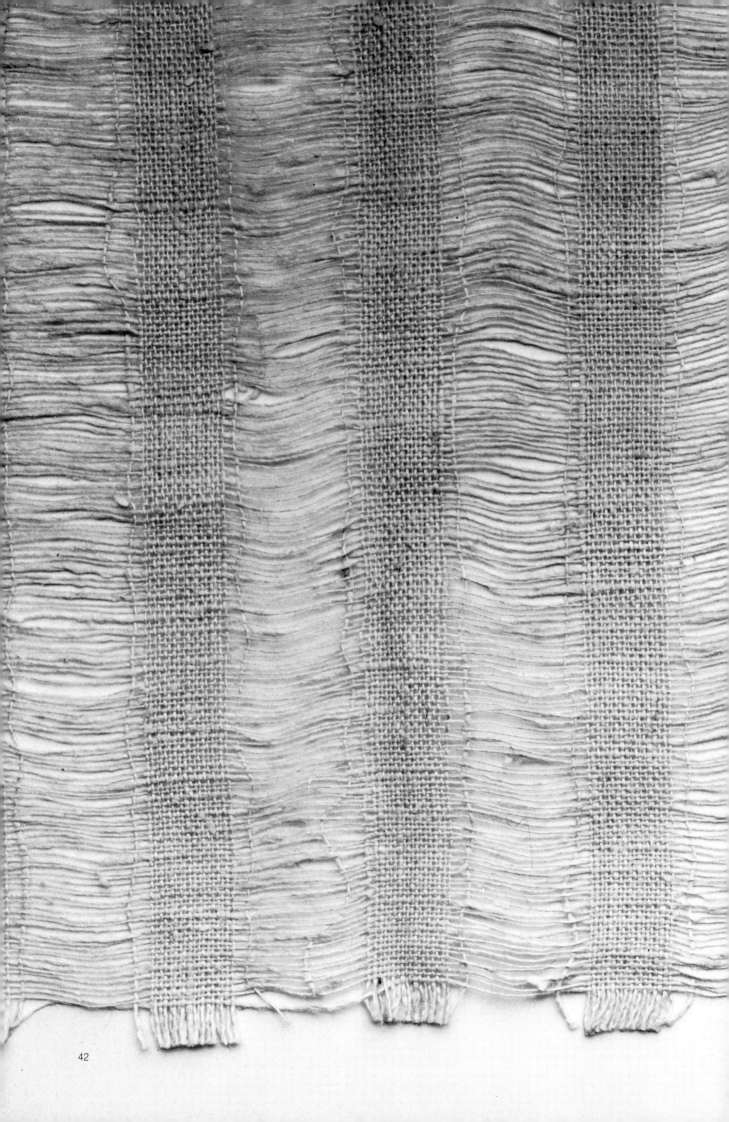

When a plain weave structure, warp and/or weft, has bands of threads crammed closely together, followed by other threads spaced well apart (controlled by the reed in the warp, and by careful control of the beating in the weft) the openwork result is called 'cramming-and-spacing'. This is often used when an open structure is required without loss of weight or strength. It is also used where the effects of thin and dense areas are shown to advantage against light, for example, in scarves and in curtains. Sometimes, when weaving in cotton or linen, or other smooth yarns, the threads tend to wander from the edge of the crammed areas into the spaces, spoiling the crisp appearance. This can be corrected by planning to edge the densely crammed stripes with a textured thread which will stay in place.

Both these linen textiles are in plain weave, and both rely on spaces left in the reed for their design.
1. Balanced weave stripes produce a more casual effect as edge threads stray in between the spaces. (A.S.)
2. Tightly crammed groups of 4 ends tend to stay in place. (A.S.)

1   2

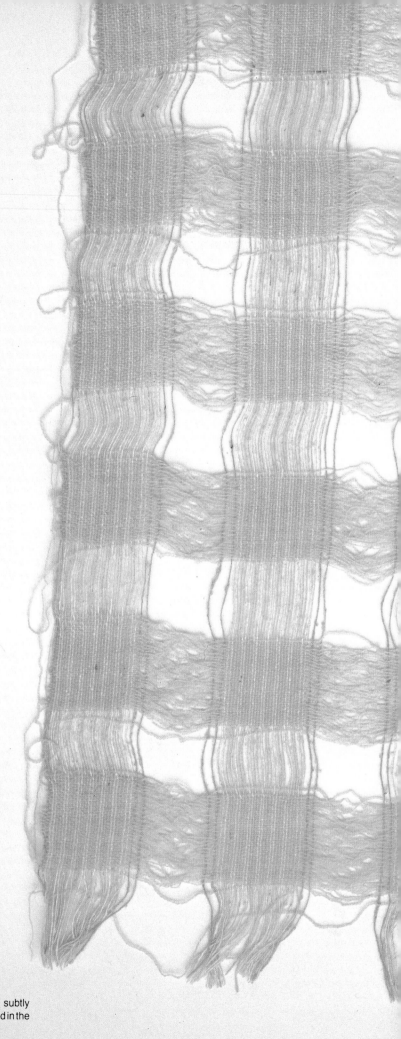

The spaces in this warp are of equal size to the bands of subtly striped silk noil. The weft, of overspun worsted wool, is spaced in the same way. (Julia Ford)

When yarns are spun, the fibres can be twisted in the same direction as the stroke in the middle of the letter S, or the letter Z (see Figs. 1 and 2).When these S- or Z-twist yarns are used in the same fabric, curious, almost indefinable, effects are seen. The cloth can be patterned with stripes, for instance, which are not caused by either weave or colour variation, but are formed by the play of light and the degree and direction of twist in the yarn.

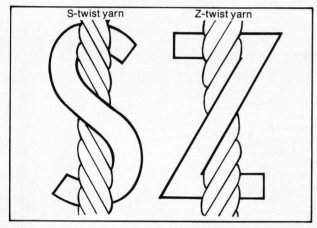

S-twist yarn   Z-twist yarn

Fig. 1   Fig. 2

Plain weave black worsted suiting cloth, where the subtle checks are formed by the use of bands of S- and Z-twist yarns in warp and weft. (Made in Huddersfield, Yorkshire, England c. 1970 and lent by West Surrey College of Art and Design)

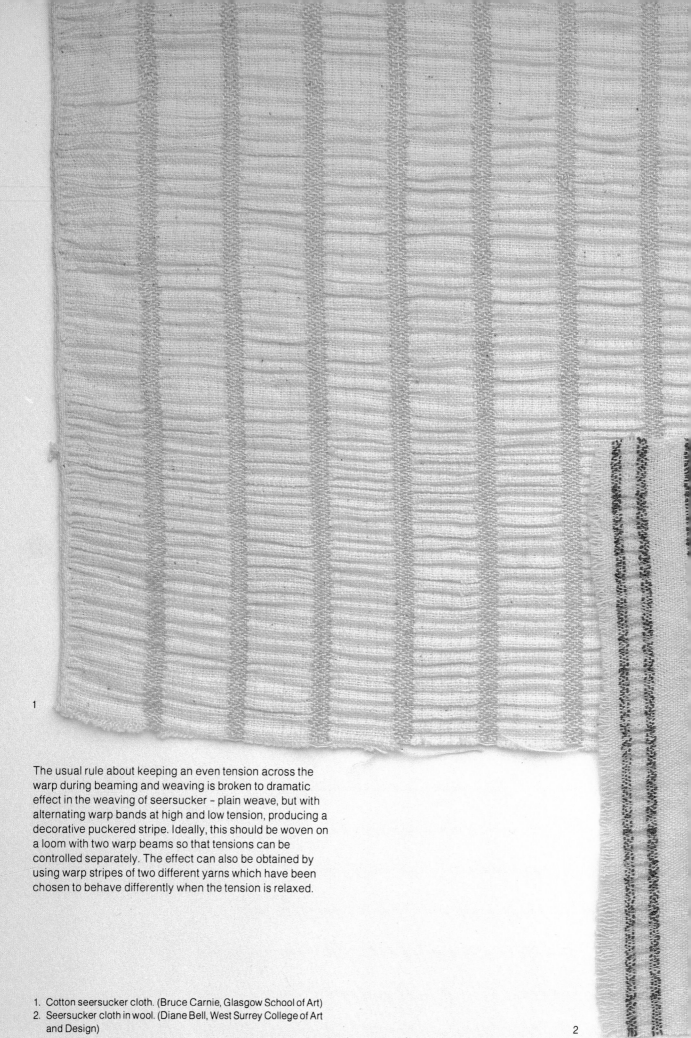

1

The usual rule about keeping an even tension across the warp during beaming and weaving is broken to dramatic effect in the weaving of seersucker – plain weave, but with alternating warp bands at high and low tension, producing a decorative puckered stripe. Ideally, this should be woven on a loom with two warp beams so that tensions can be controlled separately. The effect can also be obtained by using warp stripes of two different yarns which have been chosen to behave differently when the tension is relaxed.

1. Cotton seersucker cloth. (Bruce Carnie, Glasgow School of Art)
2. Seersucker cloth in wool. (Diane Bell, West Surrey College of Art and Design)

2

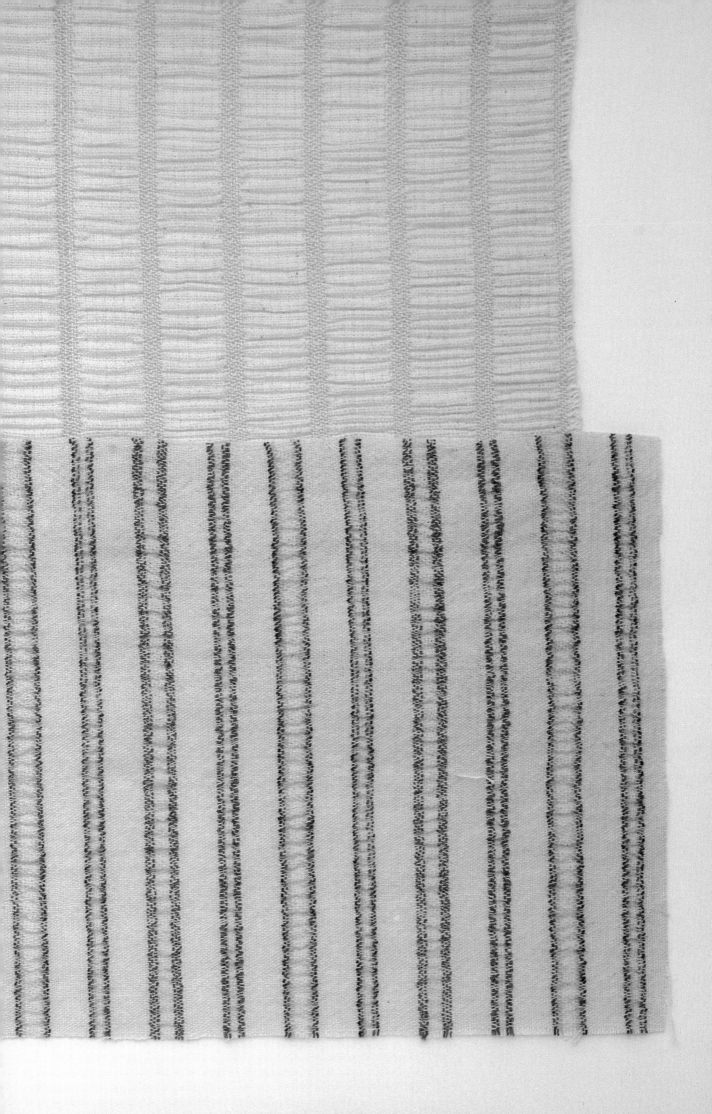

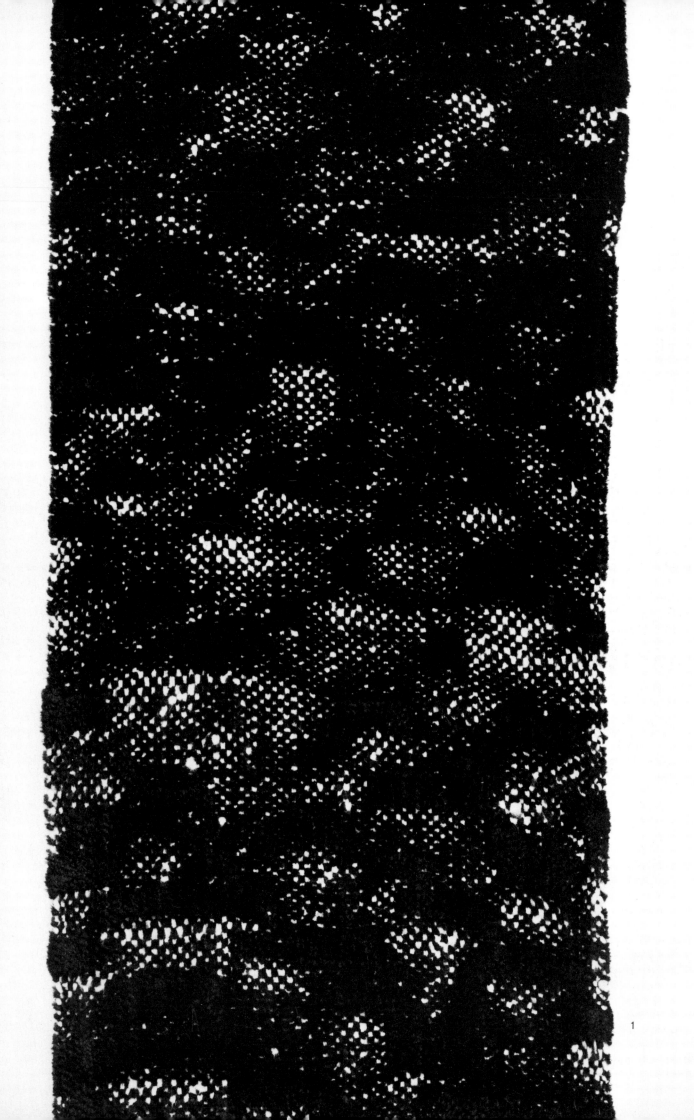

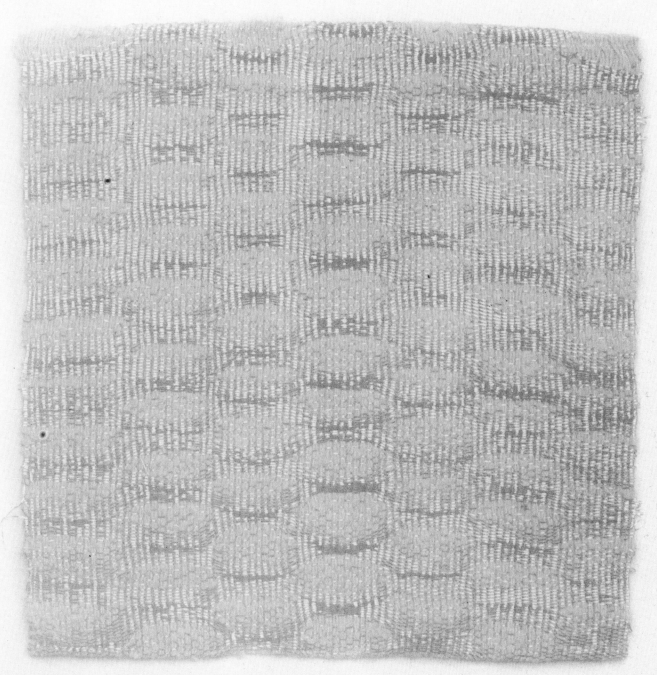

Altering the tension, in this case alternating high and low tensions on warp bands, can cause the weft to distort in a plain weave so that the warp is sometimes covered and sometimes revealed. If the warp is tensioned at random points, and these points changed at short intervals, irregular groupings of weft, combined with patches of warp exposure, occur. Elaborate equipment is not necessary for this plain weave variation. The cloths illustrated were woven with the aid of a broomstick woven in and out of groups of threads behind the heddles. The broomstick was pushed back to sit on the warp bar, where it temporarily tensioned some bands of warp more than others.

1. Plain weave: silk noil warp, silk chenille weft. Random quantities of warp yarns tensioned and released, cluster the weft picks unevenly over the cloth. (A.S.)
2. Plain weave: silk noil warp, lurex weft. Even quantities of warp yarns tensioned and released to cluster and space the weft. (A.S.)

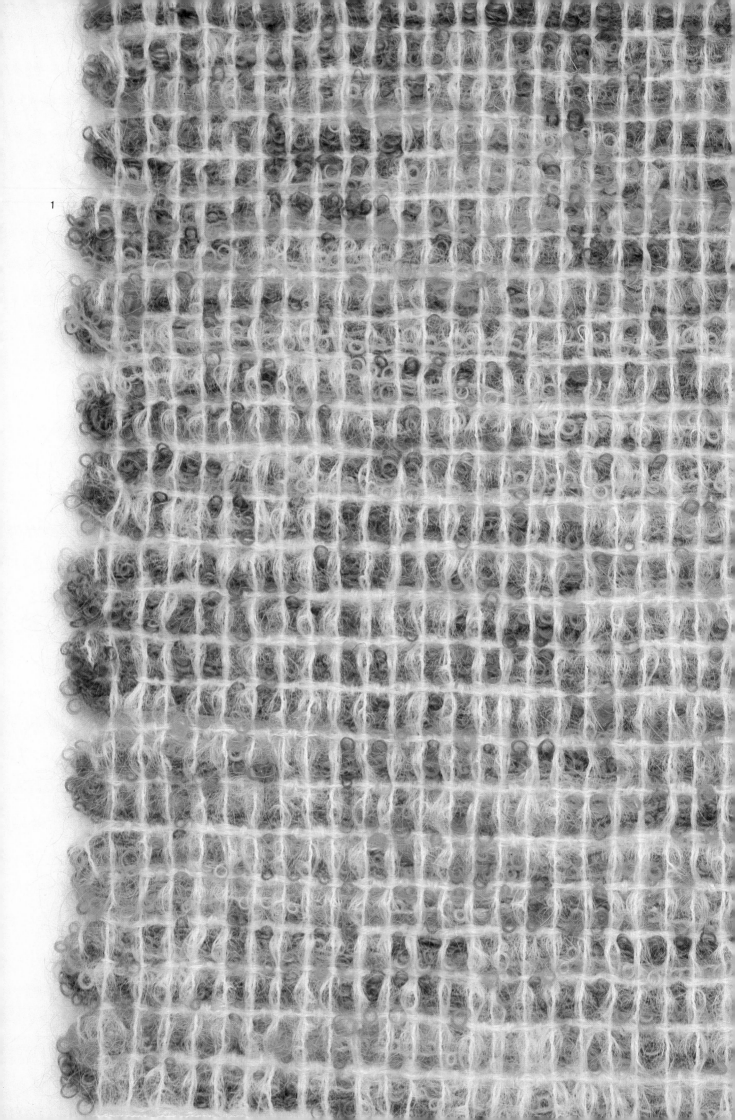

1

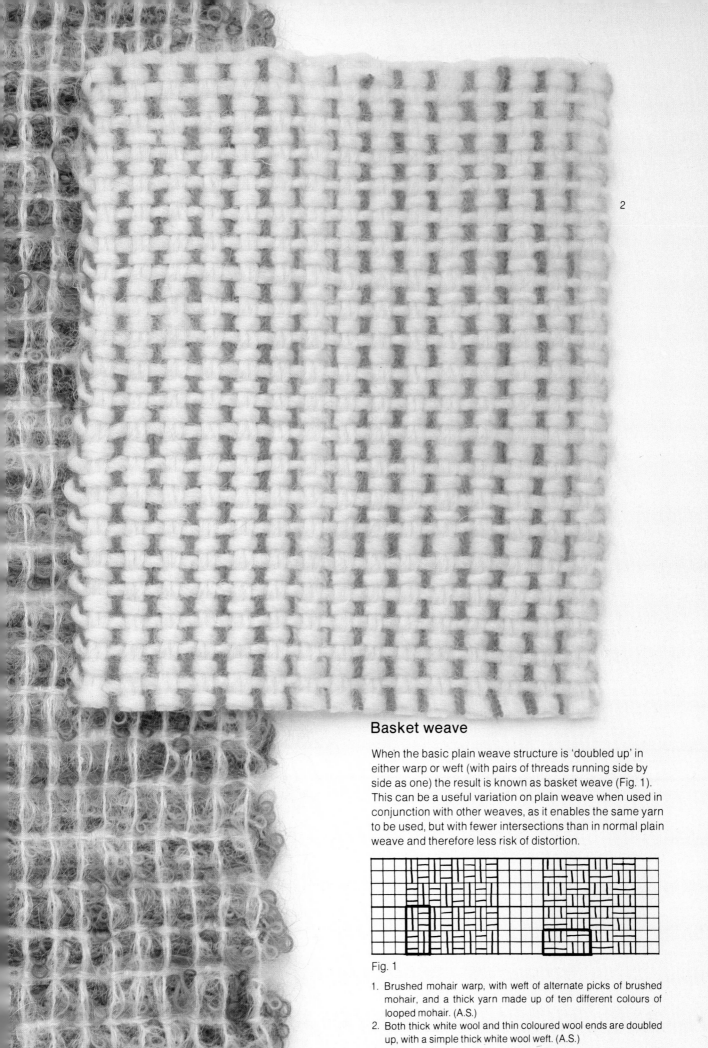

2

Basket weave

When the basic plain weave structure is 'doubled up' in either warp or weft (with pairs of threads running side by side as one) the result is known as basket weave (Fig. 1). This can be a useful variation on plain weave when used in conjunction with other weaves, as it enables the same yarn to be used, but with fewer intersections than in normal plain weave and therefore less risk of distortion.

Fig. 1

1. Brushed mohair warp, with weft of alternate picks of brushed mohair, and a thick yarn made up of ten different colours of looped mohair. (A.S.)
2. Both thick white wool and thin coloured wool ends are doubled up, with a simple thick white wool weft. (A.S.)

Another variation on plain weave is to build up the numbers of ends and/or picks running together to form thicker threads from the same yarn as that used for the body of the cloth. This adds weight to the fabric, as well as a decorative element, and it can affect the fabric's draping qualities. Grouping threads in the weft, for example, will give a stiffer 'fold' to a cloth when hung.

Grouping threads in the warp may help the draping qualities. These threads may be treated in two different ways. Each thread may be entered in a separate heddle on the same shaft, and sleyed normally, which will give a flat band of warp threads working side by side. Alternatively the grouped warp threads may be entered as one thick thread on one heald, which results in a rounded cord in the warp. These two methods can be used effectively in the same cloth.

1. Gradually increasing groups of threads in the weft, 2, 4, 6, 8, 10, then reversing back to 2 again. Wool. (A.S.)
2. 8 ends grouped as one, with a double thread running down the centre of the stripe between. Wool. (Lent by West Surrey College of Art and Design)
3. Three threads acting as one, alternating with a single pick, are beaten so that they amount to the same number per inch (2.5 cm) as in the warp. Wool. (P. Trock, Denmark, lent by West Surrey College of Art and Design)

Overleaf:
Hopsack scarf in silk. (Julia Ford)

54

3

1

2

3

Hopsack

When both warp and weft threads act in pairs in enlarged plain weave interlacement, the cloth is called 'hopsack'. The character of a hopsack cloth, like a cloth of any structure, varies according to the yarns and sett used. These examples show tough cowhair/loop mohair furnishing cloths in hopsack, and soft mohair garment fabrics, showing colour-and-weave patterning on a hopsack base. Both hopsack and basket-weave have fewer interlacements than plain weave and therefore produce a more flexible cloth. However, no more than the original 2 shafts are needed (Fig. 1).

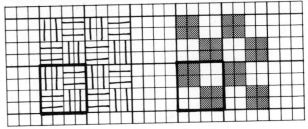

Fig. 1

1. Looped and brushed mohair hopsack. (A.S.)
2. Upholstery fabric in hopsack: cowhair yarn. (A.S.)
3. Brushed mohair hopsack.

1

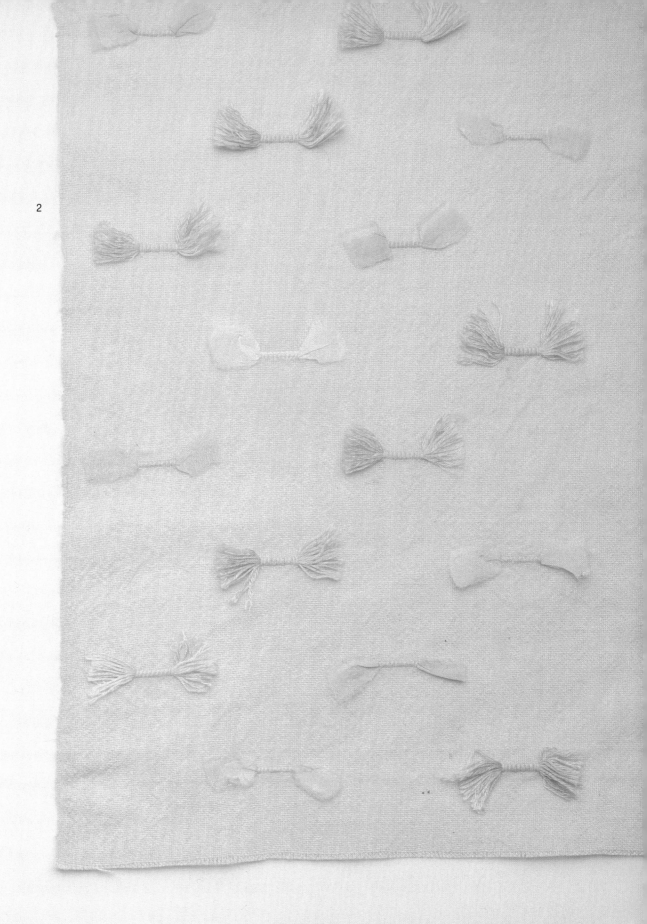

2

Plain weave can be embellished in hand-weaving by means of manual techniques such as inlay, brocading, or the insertion of material under small areas of warp.

1. Sample for a silk shawl, with very fine inlaid areas. (Melanie Spira, West Surrey College of Art and Design)
2. Lengths of silk fabric and bunches of silk threads tucked under some warp threads during weaving. (Klair Casey, West Surrey College of Art and Design)

Plain weave can be altered in character by using closely sett fine warp and alternating thick and thin weft.

1. Jute warp almost covering thick unspun coir alternating with jute weft. (A.S.)
2. Alternating colours in the thin cotton warp are shown, or concealed, by alternating very thick and very thin weft threads. (Veronica Volpicelli, Central School of Art and Design, London)

1

2

Plain weave, like any weave, can be enriched by the colouring of warp and/or weft. This can be arranged so that the colours are applied to the yarns in certain areas only. When woven, patterns emerge which are caused by these coloured areas only and not by any complex weave.

The yarns can be dyed with some parts obscured from the dye, in random or planned fashion. This technique has different names in different parts of the world. A common name is warp or weft 'ikat', with the term 'double ikat' being applied to a cloth in which both warp **and** weft have areas selected to resist the dye. (This is usually done by binding something impervious, for example raffia or plastic, round the areas which are to resist the dye.) In some weft or double ikats the weft is adjusted at the selvedges in order to produce a clear image in the finished cloth.

Silk ikat ribbons. (Muniza Khan, Loughborough College of Art and Design.)

Overleaf:
Bold double ikat in wool and mohair cloth. (Alison Gage, Central School of Art and Design, London)

65

1

2

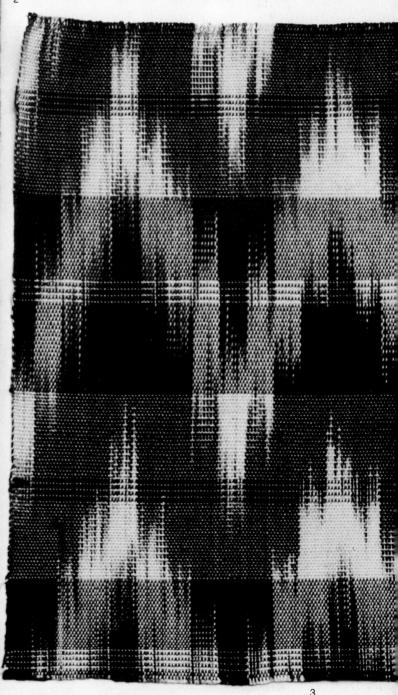

1. Warp-face cloth in silk with ikat stripes. Plain weave. (Penny Ephson, West Surrey College of Art and Design)
2. Plain weave, space-dyed (indigo) wool in warp and weft. (Jane Martin, lent by West Surrey College of Art and Design)
3. Plain weave, indigo-dyed cotton, warp ikat with weft stripes. (Kerry Stokes, West Surrey College of Art and Design)

Previous page:
1. Weft ikat, silk sari. (India)
2. Double ikat, silk sari. (India, lent by Anne Fewlass)

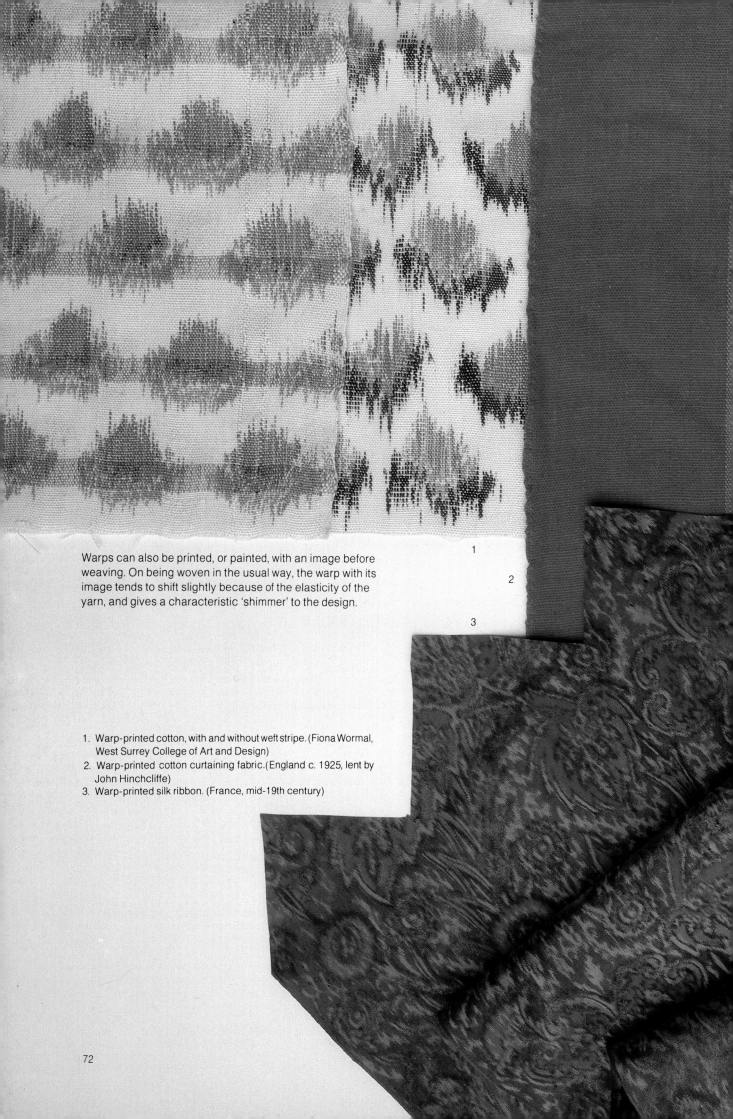

Warps can also be printed, or painted, with an image before weaving. On being woven in the usual way, the warp with its image tends to shift slightly because of the elasticity of the yarn, and gives a characteristic 'shimmer' to the design.

1. Warp-printed cotton, with and without weft stripe. (Fiona Wormal, West Surrey College of Art and Design)
2. Warp-printed cotton curtaining fabric.(England c. 1925, lent by John Hinchcliffe)
3. Warp-printed silk ribbon. (France, mid-19th century)

Two printed warps, with different patterns, can be interspersed in stripes. In this example, one of the patterns is woven in basket weave, the other in plain weave. Only 2 shafts should be necessary in theory, although in practice the warp will be distributed over many more in order to accommodate the number of ends per inch (2.5 cm), and to reduce friction on the warp ends as they pass one another.

Silk shawl. (Mid-19th century)

Twills

Twills are the second most important group of weaves after plain weave. Whereas all the variations of the plain weave structure can be woven on 2 shafts, at least 3 shafts are needed in order to weave twill. Some elaborate twills can need as many as 32 shafts.

In simple, or ordinary, twill the points of intersection in the weave move one sideways and one upwards on every pick. Characteristic diagonal lines are formed on the cloth, which may be from bottom right to top left or vice versa. However, the direction on one side of the cloth is always opposite to that on the reverse side.

Reasons for choosing a twill weave. A twill weave will result in a firm but flexible cloth with a more subtle handle than the same yarns would give in plain weave. For clothing, a carefully sett cloth in twill will hang well and softly. For this reason it is the weave most commonly used for tweeds. Used as a furnishing fabric, it will drape well in curtains, ease smoothly over upholstery and help rugs to lie flat and heavily. This is because more yarn can be packed into a weft-faced twill than into a plain weave, thus giving the desired weight in the rug.

A twill is called **plain**, or **regular**, when the ordering of interlacing is simple and unvaried and the diagonals are continuous.

When the interlacing is over and under the same number of threads, the twill is called **even**. For example, 2/2 twill and 3/3 twill; drafts shown in Figs. 1 and 2.

Uneven twills pass over larger or smaller numbers of threads than they pass under. For example 2/1 twill, 3/1 twill and 3/2 twill; drafts shown in Figs. 3, 4 and 5.

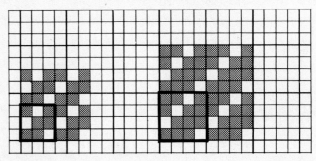

Fig. 3   Fig. 4

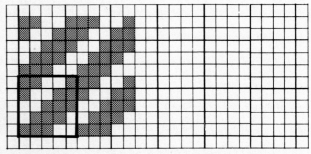

Fig. 5

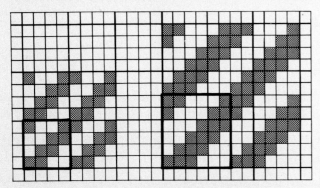

Fig. 1   Fig. 2

Two different weights of cloth in the same twill weave.
1. Travel rug, hand-spun wool, 2/2 twill. (M. Curnow, West Surrey College of Art and Design)
2. Silk twill hat ribbon. (Mid-19th century)

1

2

Three-end twills

Although this is the simplest of the twills, it is not the one most commonly used by hand-weavers as the use of 3 shafts restricts the use of the warp for any other weave, including plain. It is commonly used in industry for most denims. An old name for the weave is, in fact, 'jean'. It is an uneven twill, and so produces a warp-face fabric on one side, and a weft-face fabric on the other. There are four ways in which it can be woven (Figs. 1–4).

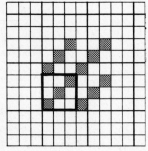

Fig. 1

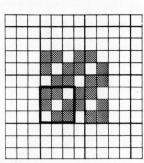

Fig. 2

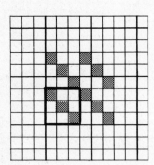

Fig. 3

Fig. 4

Fig. 1 is the reverse side of Fig. 2, and Fig. 3 is the reverse side of Fig. 4. The twill, therefore, can run from right to left or vice versa, and either one-third or two-thirds of warp or weft can be on the surface. Horizontal stripes of all four variations are, of course, possible on the same threading by varying the lifting, and the order of lifting.

1. & 2. 2/1 twill cloths with colour-and-weave patterning.
3. 2/1 twill cloth.
4. Cloth including all four variations of 2/1 twill.

3

4

79

2

3

Four-end twills

1

There are six variations of the two basic twills, 2/2 and 3/1, which can be woven on 4 ends (and 4 shafts) (Figs. 1–6).

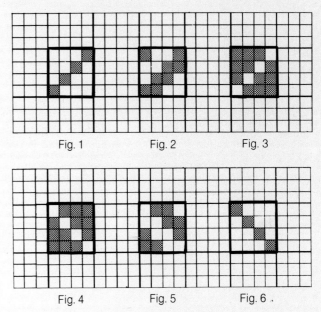

Fig. 1   Fig. 2   Fig. 3

Fig. 4   Fig. 5   Fig. 6 .

One of the most popular weaves, second only to plain, is the 2/2 twill. It is an **even** twill, and so results in the same proportion of warp and weft showing on both sides of the cloth. It is the most popular weave for traditional tweeds such as Harris, as it gives a flexible cloth which tailors well if properly sett. There is also an absence of floats which would impair the hard-wearing qualities needed. These tweeds are usually made of singles yarn with the twist designed to bed in with the diagonal of the twill to give a firm fabric. So called 'thornproof' tweeds are woven with a two-fold yarn, again matching the angle of the fold to the angle of the diagonal.

1. 3/1 twill curtain fabric using dyed and plied woollen and worsted yarns. (Jean Cawrey, West Surrey College of Art and Design)
2. 3/1 twill with, on the right-hand side, every fourth end coloured. Woven with every fourth pick coloured. (Lent by West Surrey College of Art and Design)
3. 2/2 twill upholstery in cowhair and mohair loop. (A.S.)

Five-end twills

The use of 5 shafts makes it possible to weave three twill weaves plus their 'opposites', as well as the same weaves twilling in the opposite direction (Figs. 1-6).

Six-end twills

With the use of 6 shafts, the number of twills possible rises to eight (5 different interlacings, and 3 'opposites') (Figs. 7-14).

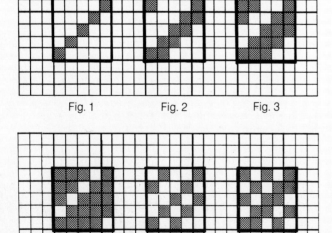

Fig. 1   Fig. 2   Fig. 3

Fig. 4   Fig. 5   Fig. 6

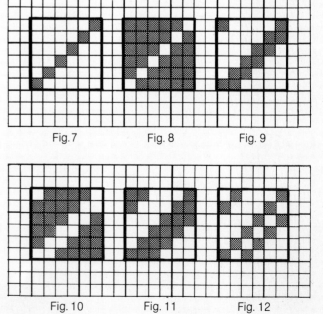

Fig. 7   Fig. 8   Fig. 9

Fig. 10   Fig. 11   Fig. 12

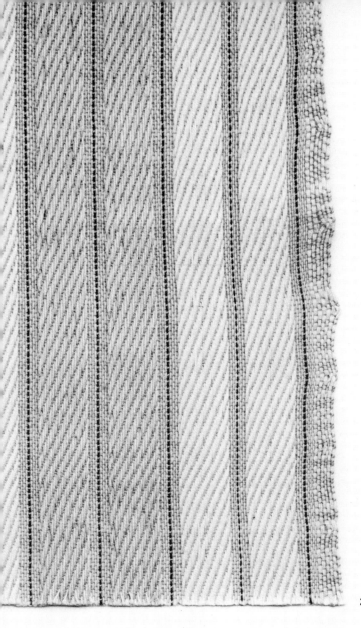

2

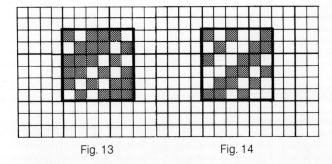

Fig. 13   Fig. 14

All these are uneven twills except for Fig. 11, the classic and much used 3/3 twill. They can all, of course, be inclined in the opposite direction as well.

With an 8-shaft loom, 2 shafts are still available for warp bands (or selvedges) of plain weave or hopsack if required. The use of hopsack, which has fewer intersections than plain weave, will reduce the risk of tight and slack bands in the cloth.

Care must be taken when floats are as long as 5 ends or picks, as the cloth can become sleazy. An adaptation which includes some diagonal bands of plain weave will stop this tendency.

1. 3/3 twill wool furnishing fabric. ('Supertwill', designed by Peter Simpson, R.D.I., Bute Fabrics Ltd)
2. Warp stripes of 5/1 twill and plain weave in a cotton furnishing fabric. (Kim Leigh, West Surrey College of Art and Design)

Eight-end twills

There are no advantages in using 7 shafts for a twill, although it is perfectly possible in theory to do so. However, a large group of twills are possible when 8 shafts are available. This is so large a group that it is sensible to start to work through the permutations systematically, in order to understand the principles of designing a twill structure. To start, make a single diagonal row of marks on an 8 x 8 inch square. Then add successive rows of marks to the right (Figs. 1–7).

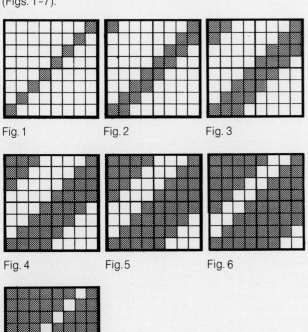

Fig. 1   Fig. 2   Fig. 3

Fig. 4   Fig. 5   Fig. 6

Fig. 7

Taking the above in turn, add another row of single marks to the right of each, wherever possible (Figs. 8–12).

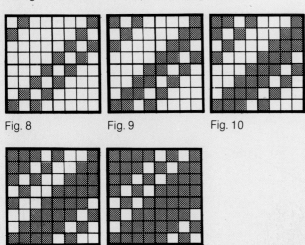

Fig. 8   Fig. 9   Fig. 10

Fig. 11   Fig. 12

Try the single marks again, but this time with a gap of two spaces (Figs. 13–16).

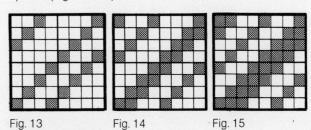

Fig. 13   Fig. 14   Fig. 15

Fig. 16

Then try three spaces away (Figs. 17, 18 and 19)

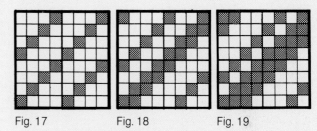

Fig. 17   Fig. 18   Fig. 19

and finally four spaces away (Figs. 20 and 21).

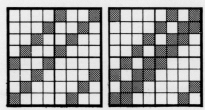

Fig. 20   Fig. 21

The process can be continued in this systematic way until all the possible twills are revealed. The next step is to weed out the duplicates. For example, in those completed so far Fig. 10 and Fig. 19 are identical. So are Fig. 11 and Fig. 16, and Fig. 9 and Fig. 21. Other pairs are opposite to one another, and would occur on the reverse side (Fig. 9 and Fig. 11; Fig. 16 and Fig 21).

Several different 8-end twills in one fabric. (Catherine Carmichael, Glasgow School of Art)

The influence of twist on twills

Few other weaves are as influenced as twills by the S or Z direction of the twist in warp and weft yarns (see page 47). The diagonal line of the twill weave can be diminished, or emphasized, by the careful use of direction combined with twist.

In any cloth where warp and weft are both the same twist, either S or Z, the yarns will bed into one another to form a compact cloth. Where the twist is different in warp and weft, one being S and the other Z, the threads will not merge with one another, and consequently the weave will be more defined.

When a twill weave is used, the prominence of the diagonals can be accentuated if their direction is in opposition to the twist of the yarn. In other words, a Z-twist warp woven in twill with diagonals rising from bottom right to top left will have prominent lines; reverse the direction and the lines will be less distinct. The twist direction of the weft will also alter the effect. However, this effect depends very much on the amount of twist in the yarns, and on the sett.

Cloth in 2/2 twill; all yarns are the same colour of natural white wool – the weave is a constant 2/2 twill in one direction. The shadow checks are formed entirely by the direction of the S- or Z-twist in the yarn, fitting in with, or opposing, the direction of the twill angle. (D. E. Lawson, West Surrey College of Art and Design)

Striped twills

When planning horizontal or vertical stripes of
different twills particular attention must be paid
to the point where the stripes join one another.
It is essential that there should be a good
'lock' to the two structures. Sometimes it may be
necessary to add an end or pick over the repeat in order to
achieve this. The results of a neat lock can be examined on
point-paper by taking, for example, a simple warp stripe of 8
ends each of alternate faces of a 3/1 twill (Fig. 1).

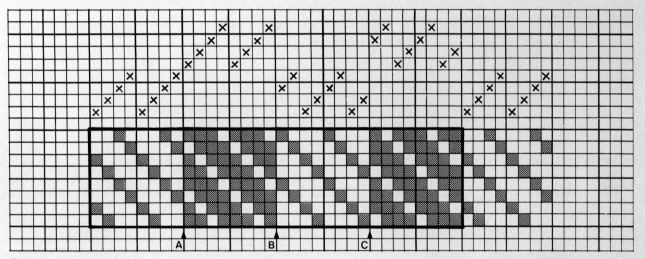

Fig. 1

The first stripe on the left is a normal straight draft, and the
join at line A is easily accomplished to lock in with the
second, warp-face stripe. However, when reverting to weft-
face for the third stripe (join B), it is necessary to break the
threading sequence, so that a crisp join is achieved. This
also happens at join C. The sequence is only back to
'normal' at the end of the fourth stripe.

The same problems occur when weaving the same twill in
weftways stripes. In this case the threading is on 4 shafts,
and is a straight draft, but the lifting sequences must stagger
on the third and fourth stripes to give a crisp join.
All this can be planned on point-paper before the warp is put
on to the loom. It will be helpful, especially when planning
stripes of very different weaves, to draw out an area of each
weave on separate pieces of point-paper and move them
against one another until the best lock is found (Fig. 2).
(Remember that it may well be different on the next join.)
Attention to this type of detail is an important part of weaving
good cloth.

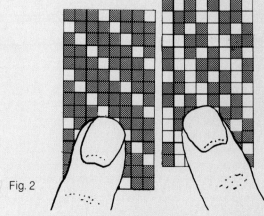

Fig. 2

1. Fancy twill showing three different weft colours on the same pink
   warp. Wool. ('Ligurie', Placide Joliet, France, sample supplied by
   Homeworks, London)
2. Warp stripes of 2/1 twill alongside stripes of 1/2 twill. Hand-spun
   yarns, natural dyes. (Margaret Hensley, West Surrey College of
   Art and Design)

1

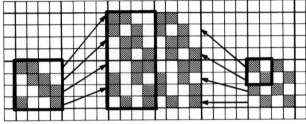

Combining weaves, only one of which may be a twill, will produce twill variations. A simple example would be 2/2 twill and plain weave, with the rows alternating in the weft (Fig. 2).

Fig 2

This also produces a steeper angle to the twill (see page 99).

Designing twills

When designing a twill fabric it is essential to remember that the more frequent the intersections, the firmer the resulting cloth will be. Twills can be written down in several ways; a point-paper draft is not necessary in order to describe a twill. It is common for the plain twills to be written as 2/2 and 3/3, or $\frac{2}{2}$ and $\frac{3}{3}$; a more elaborate twill would be written as $\frac{3\ 1}{1\ 3}$ or $\frac{5\ 1}{1\ 1}$ (Because these numbers add up to eight, the twill can be woven on 8 shafts.) In both of these examples, there are four interlacings, and they would be of similar stability when woven.

Fancy twills

The word 'fancy' has been used for a long time in cloth construction to describe any variation on the weave under discussion. A fancy twill is often a combination of two or more simple twills.

The number of shafts available should be considered constantly as it is obviously easier to work out a fancy twill if many shafts are available. Designing twills for only 4 shafts is much more difficult. Fig.1 shows a fancy twill for 4 shafts and 6 pedals. If another 2 pedals are available (or a table-loom) then plain weave is also possible.

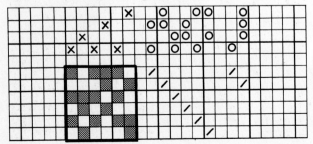

Fig 1

There are many simple 'games' to play on point-paper which will produce fancy weaves from plain ones. Twills are very well-suited to this sort of manipulation.

1. Setting down the same plain twill in two different ways, as in Figs. 3a and 3b, and taking the vertical rows alternately in pairs, produces a more elaborate twill which it is still possible to weave on 4 shafts (Fig. 3c).

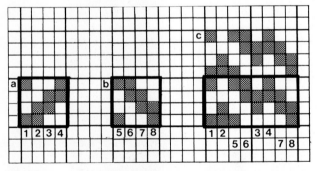

Fig. 3

By using another way of setting down exactly the same twill, Fig. 4d, and combining it with Fig. 4b again in the same way, a completely different pattern emerges (Fig. 4e).

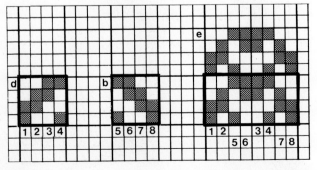

Fig. 4

2

Fig. 5 shows the result if 6 shafts are available

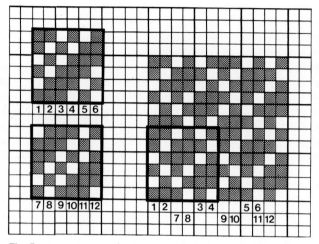

Fig. 5

and Fig. 6 8 shafts.

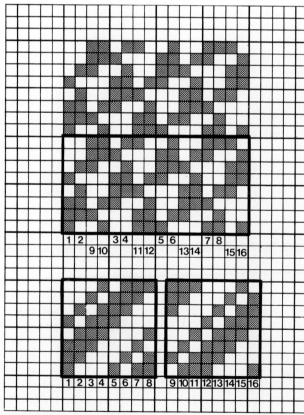

Fig. 6

There are many more weaves to be discovered using this method. Providing two different 'placings' of the same basic weave are used as starting points, the number of shafts needed for the final new weave cannot exceed the original number used for the basic weave.

2. By taking a plain twill and setting it out on alternate vertical and horizontal rows on the point-paper, and then rotating it so that the marks are set down four times, from different directions, a new weave will result (Figs. 7 and 8).

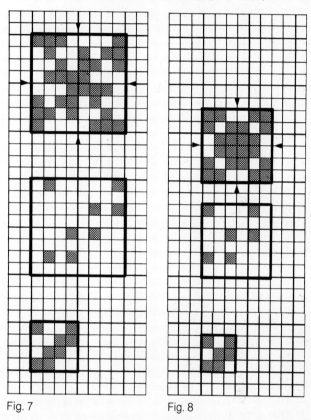

Fig. 7   Fig. 8

1. 8-shaft fancy twill spray-dyed cotton warp, worsted and lurex weft. (G. Heminsley, Glasgow School of Art)
2. 8-shaft fancy twill in coarse silk. (A.S.)
3. Alternate rows of 2/2 twill and plain weave increases the angle of the twill rib. Cowhair and loop mohair. (A.S.) The draft at Fig. 2 shows the 4-shaft fancy twill.

3

1

2

Broken twills

The insistent diagonal
emphasis of a twill
structure can be made
almost unobtrusive by
'breaking' the straight draft.
A simple way to do this is to
'remove' ends on a twill
draft. With a 2/2 twill, every
third end can be removed
(Fig. 1).

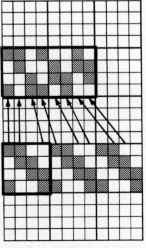

Fig. 1

The lower part of Fig. 1 shows three repeats of a 2/2 twill. Care must be taken to repeat the original weave often enough to be able to create a repeat on the 'selected' weave. Two ends are transferred to the weave above, and one end missed out, until the repeat is complete, which it will be on the Lowest Common Multiple of the original 4 ends and the selected 3 ends: 12 ends. This new weave does not have a strong diagonal appearance, but it has retained the stability and flexibility of the original twill.

Other twills, and other selections, will produce similarly 'broken' results. Fig. 2 shows the result of a 3/3 twill, broken by selecting 2, leaving 2, selecting 4 and leaving 2 ends.

1. Ecclesiastical vestment fabric in broken 3/1 twill, silk warp, cotton weft. (Anne Spaull, West Surrey College of Art and Design)
2. Dress fabric in broken 3/1 twill. Cheviot wool. (Judith Straw, West Surrey College of Art and Design)

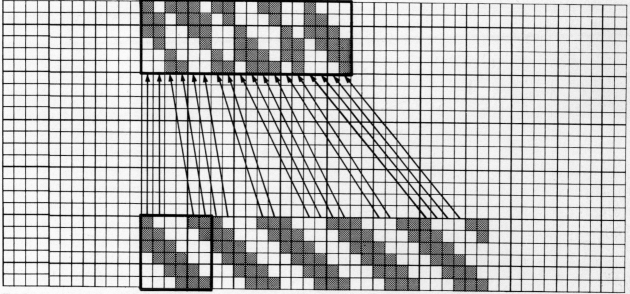

Fig. 2

2a

2b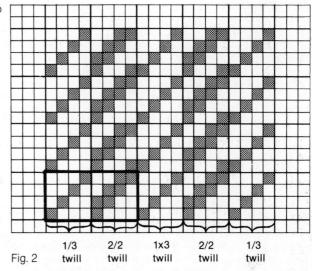

	1/3 twill	2/2 twill	1x3 twill	2/2 twill	1/3 twill

Fig. 2

Shaded twills

In some fancy twills a regular swelling occurs on the diagonal line, and this gives the appearance of a shaded area. There are other ways of achieving this effect – many are outside the 8-shaft limit of this book, but several are possible, even on 4 shafts. One of the simplest is woven on a straight draft, weaving bands of 3/1 twill, 2/2 twill, 1/3 twill, 2/2 twill in succession (Fig. 1).

Undulating twills

A twill of any type can be made to undulate across the cloth by combining it with a crammed-and-spaced warp (see page 42). Another way of undulating a twill is by using double, or even treble, groups of warp ends. The curve can be controlled by doubling or trebling ends in conjunction with single ends. This undulation can be applied to any 8-shaft twill. In theory, this would work with a 4-end twill, but the extra richness possible with 8 shafts gives a more dramatic result.

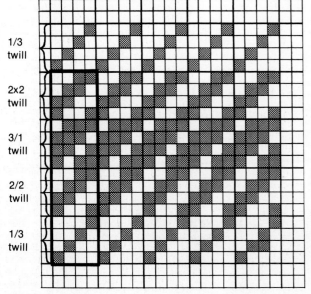

1/3 twill

2x2 twill

3/1 twill

2/2 twill

1/3 twill

Fig. 1

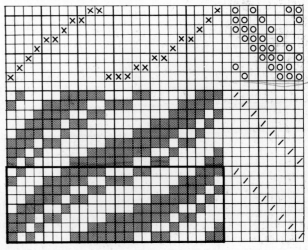

Fig. 3

When weaving this, be careful to maintain a straight edge to one side of the diagonal (in Fig. 1, the straight edge is to the right side), increasing and decreasing the shaded area from that side only. A shaded effect, using 8 shafts, can be obtained from warp stripes of 1/3 twill and 2/2 twill. Each band will, of course, need 4 shafts (Fig. 2).

1. Undulating twill cloth where this effect has been achieved by using three different thicknesses of cotton yarn in each colour stripe in the warp. (Annie Derbyshire, Central School of Art and Design, London)

2. Examples of shaded twill: (a) progressing from 3/1 twill, through 2/2 twill, to 1/3 twill, and then starting again from the beginning. (A.S.) (b) The same progression, but reversing the order of twills to return to the beginning of the weft repeat. (A.S.)

98

Altering the angle of a twill

The angle of the diagonal ribs of a twill is 45 degrees if the sett is balanced and the yarns used in warp and weft are equal in thickness (or, if they are not, are compensated for in the sett).

The angle can be made steeper by:

(a) using a thicker weft (or a thinner warp);

(b) setting the warp more closely;

(c) altering the structure. One way to do this is to take alternate ends of a twill (which may originally have needed twice the number of shafts which are available for the altered weave). (See Fig. 1a.)

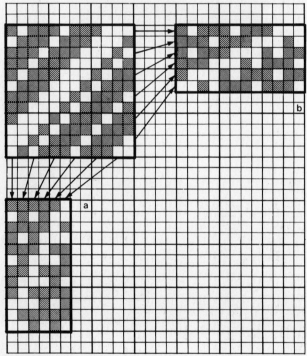

Fig. 1

The angle can be made more gradual by:
(a) using a thinner weft;
OR (b) setting the warp more openly;
OR (c) altering the structure. Alternate picks can be extracted from a multi-shaft twill. (See Fig. 1b.)

1. Two examples of the same design, a 6-end twill (in herringbone formation) showing how a change of yarn can affect the angle of the twill. The plied weft packs down to make a shallower angle, and the singles weft remains bulky and gives a steeper angle to the same twill. ('Kilbrannan Chevron', designed by Peter Simpson, R.D.I., Bute Fabrics Ltd)

2. Alternate rows of plain weave, in between the picks of 2/2 twill, extend it into a steeper angle. (A.S.)

Previous page:

1. The dramatic effect that a yarn can have on a fabric – every white weft stripe in the top half of this cloth is woven in Lycra, an elastomeric yarn, woven in tension. When released, the cloth is 'shirred' in that area. (Jill Hinds, Derby Lonsdale College)

2. Silk fabric in 7/1 twill, broken in pairs, with 2 ends of plain weave between the stripes. (Anna Cady, West Surrey College of Art and Design)

3. Woollen cloth design for shawl in alternating blocks of 2/2 twill and hopsack. (Roger Horn, West Surrey College of Art and Design)

Reverse twills, herringbones and chevrons

There is some confusion about the names of weaves which are based on twill, but whose diagonals form zigzags either vertically or horizontally.

A **reverse twill** is a weave in which the twill diagonal progresses in one direction right across the cloth during weaving, and is then reversed to progress in the opposite direction (Fig. 1).

Fig. 1

The threading is the same as for a straight twill, and the pedalling is reversed in order after a determined number of picks.

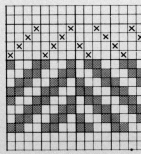

Both **herringbone and chevron twills** zigzag in the opposite direction to a reverse twill (Fig. 2).

Fig. 2

The difference between these twills lies at the vertical divisions between the twill directions. Chevron, or more accurately **point twill**, has a draft (called a point draft) which reverses without a break (Fig. 3).

Fig. 3

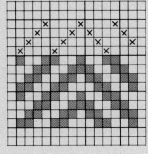

This, however, causes a point of weakness where a pick crosses over 3 ends, and for a firmer fabric, a herringbone is preferable (Fig. 4).

Fig. 4

In herringbone, at the point where the draft reverses (on the vertical line, or 'spine,' of the herring's backbone), some shafts are missed out to give a clean break.

Obviously, if the direction of the diagonals can be reversed in either direction, it is possible to reverse them in **both** directions and form a herringbone or chevron check. For the same structural reasons, a herringbone check is preferable, but the cleaner decorative effect of a chevron check may be preferred, particularly if the check repeats over only a few ends.

Some 'fancy' versions are produced by combinations of point draft and straight draft (Fig. 5).

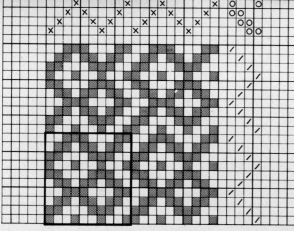

Fig. 5

1. 3/3 twill in herringbone, with a staggered vertical division. This woollen cloth has been heavily milled to felt the fibres together, ensuring stability for an upholstery fabric. ('Montana,' Placide Joliet, France, sample supplied by Homeworks, London)
2 3/1 twill herringbone dress fabric in wool and silk. (Kerry Stokes, West Surrey College of Art and Design)

1

2

1. Herringbone check dress fabric in Welsh wool. (Jane Martin, West Surrey College of Art and Design)
2. Table linen in half-bleached and unbleached yarn: 3/1 twill reversing to 1/3 twill and changing direction both warp-and weft-ways, with a staggered break. (Finland)
3. Herringbone check dress fabric in cheviot wool with the coloured check coinciding with the weave, but not repeating for six colour stripes. (Mary Jane Hall, West Surrey College of Art and Design)

Overleaf:
White worsted wool shawl with twill and granite weave blocks (see page 125) – the twill changing direction on a multi-dyed silk pick. Although this shawl was woven on 12 shafts, similar effects could be obtained using 8 shafts or less. (Julia Ford)

1. Two examples of twill and plain weave in alternating blocks in a coloured check fabric. One is more dramatically patterned than the other because the twill has been placed on the areas of the coloured check where one colour crosses the other, while the self-coloured squares carry the plain weave. (Pat Holtom)
2. 3/1 twill bands in the weft, using a thicker yarn, than in the plain weave body of the cloth. ('Scorpio', designed by Peter Simpson, R.D.I., Bute Fabrics Ltd)

Using two weaves together in the same fabric can lead to problems of tension. But if the yarns are slightly elastic, for example, wool, and the cloth is not closely sett, problems are less likely to occur. Often any cockling caused by the use of so-called 'incompatible' weaves in such cloths will be eliminated in the finishing process.

1

2

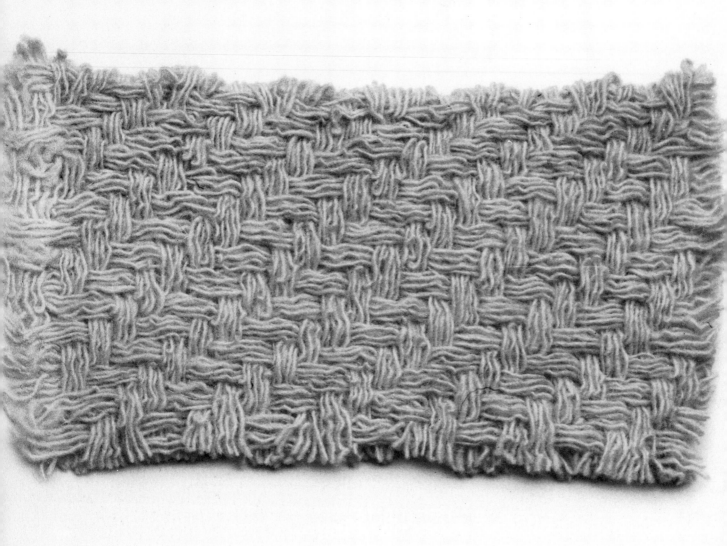

2/2 twill, with each 'thread' composed of 6 strands of Welsh wool. Fabric shown before and after heavy milling, which has felted the wool fibres together to make a stable fabric. (Anne Bagshaw, West Surrey College of Art and Design)

Previous page:
1. 2/2 twill herringbone in a 'four brown, four blue-grey', rough linen check. (Julia Ford)
Two silk fabrics inspired by birds' feathers.
2. 2/2 point twill in silk, crammed-and-spaced to undulate, warp painted. (Gail Taylor, West Surrey College of Art and Design)
3. 8-end twill herringbone reversed to form the 'eye' of a peacock feather – silk, dip-dyed and painted. (Gail Taylor, West Surrey College of Art and Design)

Overleaf:
This fancy twill – a 5/3 twill with each pick separated by two rows of plain weave – is enhanced by the use in the weft of a hand-spun yarn which includes bits of sewing cotton and printed cloth cuttings along with dyed fleece. (Catherine Carmichael, Glasgow School of Art)

111

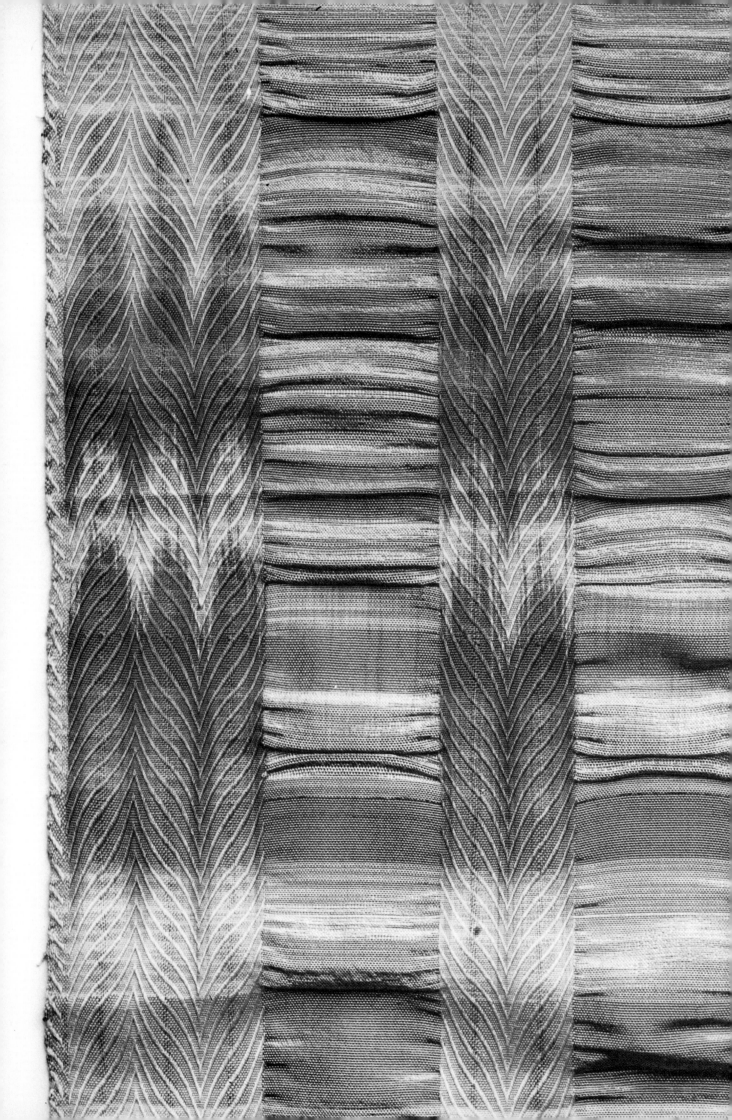

This cotton and rayon cloth includes many design features: seersucker and plain weave bands, alternating with chevron bands (crammed-and-spaced to give undulation); weft stripes (showing in the seersucker bands), and ikat-dyed warp. (Jill Richardson, Manchester Polytechnic)

115

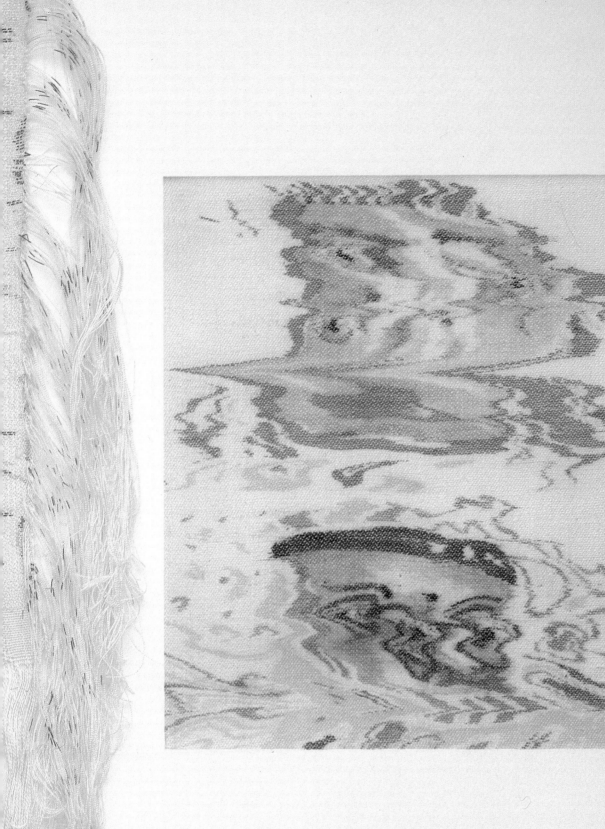

Two panels using the same technique: a fine cloth is woven then a
coloured image is drawn on it. Another warp is set up and the first
cloth is undone, pick by pick, and the threads woven into the new
warp in the right order. (The structure is broken twill.) It is possible to
pull the threads to right or left during weaving so that the image
becomes distorted. The panel on the left started off as straight
vertical coloured lines; the one on the right as a self-portrait. (June
Lillico, Glasgow School of Art)

2/2 twill used in a rug. Twill is popular for rug-weaving because it packs down well in a weft-faced structure. All weft colour-and-weave patterns are possible, as can be seen here – various combinations of black and white picks make different patterns. Plain weave bands in mercerised cotton divide the twill stripes. (Anna Crutchley, West Surrey College of Art and Design)

119

Satins

The word 'satin' is popularly used to describe a fabric with a very smooth and slippery surface, often used for evening wear, and it is difficult at first to see how this relates to cloth structures used in hand-weaving. But the word indicates a certain way of 'breaking' a twill in order to present as smooth a surface as possible, showing no apparent weave. In the case of satin it is a warp-faced weave; sateen is the weft-faced equivalent. The twill from which the weave is derived is staggered and broken as much as possible so that no diagonal, or indeed any other line, is apparent. Although 'mock satin' is possible on 4 shafts, this is really a broken twill; true satins need upwards of 5 shafts.

Satin can provide a very strong fabric, warpways. The infrequent interlacing means that the warp can be sett very closely. Often glossy threads are chosen for a satin warp because the weave will show off this quality in a yarn, as each end will lie on the surface for at least 4 picks. For this reason, any cloth which is to have a practical purpose ought to be made with a fine weft or the floats will be too long to be functionally acceptable. The nature of the structure and the probability that it will be used with a close-sett warp, make it ideal for intensely coloured warp stripes. These are often used alternately with stripes of plain weave, and will help the draping qualities of the cloth.

When the weave is turned round and becomes weft-faced it is called 'sateen'. In theory, the reverse side of a satin cloth should be sateen. In structural terms it is, but it very rarely gives the appearance of being so. This is because almost all satins are sett closely, and this unbalanced cloth will not show off a sateen weave to advantage. If a sateen surface is required, the warp should be sett comparatively openly. Often, for example in damask, areas of both satin and sateen weave are used in the same cloth. The cloth is then balanced so that neither face is eclipsed by the other.

1. Rainbow stripes in satin weave alternating with plain weave stripes. Wool. (A.S.)
2. Alternating warp stripes of satin and sateen. Linen. (Finland)

1

2

1

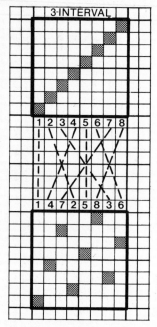

Fig. 2   Fig. 3

To construct a satin weave

In order to work out how to break up the definite line of a twill **as much as possible**, this simple rule should be followed. **Divide the number of ends (or shafts) on which the satin, or sateen, is to be woven into two unequal parts, so that one shall not be a measure of the other, nor shall it be divisible by a common number.** (This rule is impossible to apply perfectly to either 4 or 6 ends.) The numbers obtained will indicate the 'interval' which can be used.

5-end satin can have an interval of 2 or 3.
7-end satin can have an interval of 2 or 5, 3 or 4.
8-end satin can have an interval of 3 or 5.

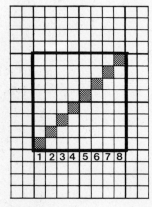

Use these numbers like this: to produce, for instance, an 8-end satin the intervals can be 3 or 5. First, put down a 7/1 twill. The 'ties' will progress diagonally from one corner to the other (Fig. 1). (Note at this stage that it is usually easier to weave satins upside down on the loom to avoid lifting the majority of the warp threads for each pick. The drafts have been shown in the sateen position with weft predominating.)

Fig. 1

This regular progression of the ties will make obvious lines across the cloth. They must be re-arranged so that they are as far apart from one another as possible. This can be accomplished by placing each vertical row, or end, 3 (or 5) rows from its previous neighbour (Figs. 2 and 3). This produces a smooth surface.

5-end satin, with intervals of 2 or 3, would work out as illustrated below (Figs. 4 and 5).

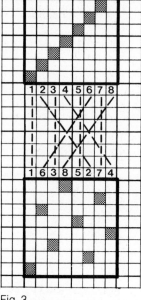

Fig. 4   Fig. 5

Sometimes it is necessary to use the 'imperfect' satins on 4 or 6 shafts. Figs. 6 and 7 show two possible rearrangements. (4-end satin is more usually regarded as a broken twill.)

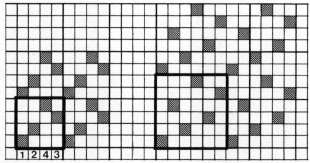

Fig. 6   Fig. 7

1. Satin ground with sateen spots. Silk. (Early 20th century)
2. Satin and twill striped dress fabric. Silk. (Mid-19th century)

2

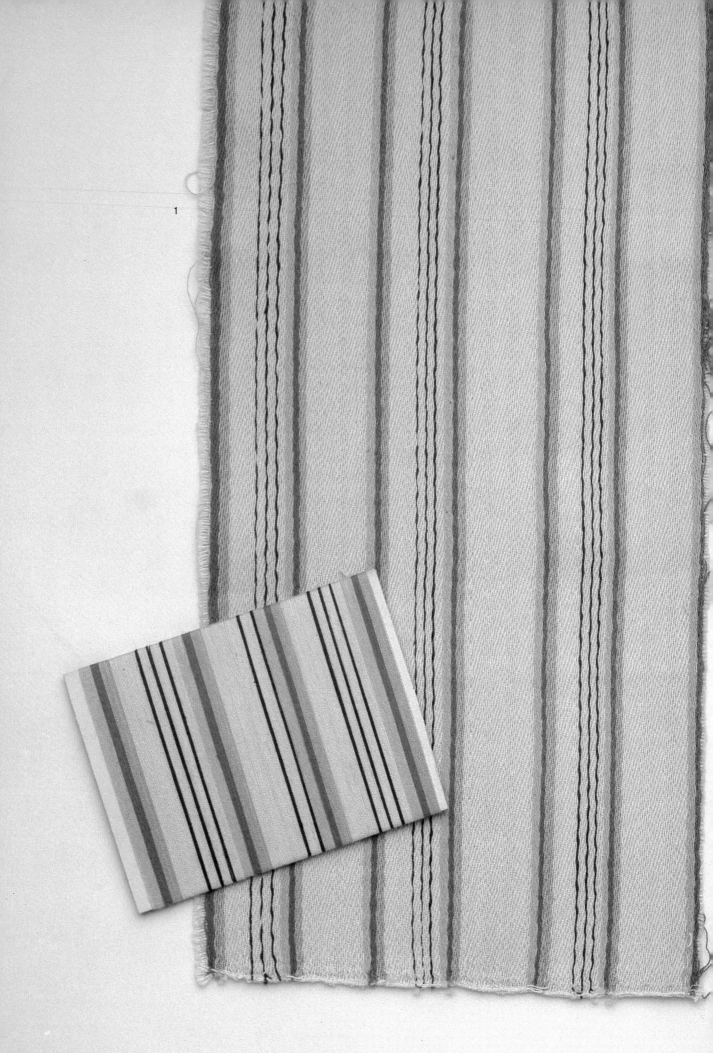

Using a satin base to evolve new weaves

An interesting use of the distribution of the 'ties' in the satin weave is that they can be used as the starting point for endless weaves of an 'all-over texture' type.

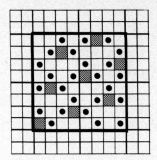

Taking an 8-end satin (this one is 3-interval), add marks to each of the tie points (Fig. 1). In this case marks have been added to the top, left and right of each tie.

Fig. 1

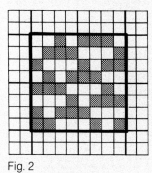

When these marks become 'warp up', an all-over weave results which can be woven on a straight draft of 8 shafts (Fig. 2). This particular weave has weft emphasis (the longest floats are in the weft). If a warp emphasis is preferred, then the draft can be turned round at this stage.

Fig. 2

The satin ties can also be used as the starting points of twill sequences. One line of a twill is put down and repeated, starting each time on the satin tie-point (Fig. 3).

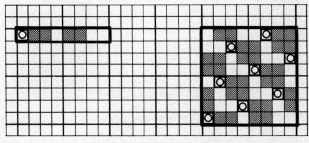

Fig. 3

Another way of obtaining the same result would be to set down the twill and transpose the lines on a satin 'interval'.

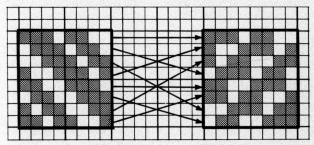

Fig. 4

These all-over weaves, derived from a satin basis, are sometimes called 'granites', and are widely used for tweeds or other fabrics where an all-over small-scale texture weave is needed. In contrast to the source of their derivation, they supply, as the name implies, a visually granular surface.

2

1. Striped satin in cotton. This was designed by winding yarns around a card, and then by weaving a sample with the stripes in the weft so that the proportions could be adjusted before a striped warp was set up. (Anna Radley, West Surrey College of Art and Design)
2. Three 'granite' weaves.

1. Coarse furnishing satin in natural wools. (A.S.)
2. Worsted furnishing fabric in chequerboard squares of satin and sateen. The colour changes on every third band warpways and sometimes halfway through a block weftways, giving a larger and more elaborate pattern repeat. (Pat Holtom)
3. Wool curtain fabric in plain weave with stripes of irregular satin. ('Ardmore', designed by Peter Simpson, R.D.I., Bute Fabrics Ltd)

Floats

float depends primarily on the thickness of thread being used in the base cloth, and its sett. The proposed use of the cloth must also be considered; floats of a few inches may be acceptable on a nonfunctional hanging, but could make a garment cloth unusable. The choice of fibre also plays a part in determining the practical length of a float. For example, it is possible to felt down a woollen yarn float so that it adheres to both the base cloth and its neighbours in the finishing process.

When a thread passes over several others, it is called a skip or float. This can occur in warp and weft, or both. It is frequently used as a decorative device to enrich a plain weave ground. When planning this sort of cloth, care has to be taken that floats do not reach impractical lengths. The number of threads over which another thread may safely

A yarn may float on both sides of a cloth, merely passing through the base cloth at intervals without taking a structural role. It may also weave into the cloth between floats. In the former case, floating yarns of a very different nature from the base can be used without affecting the sett to any great extent.

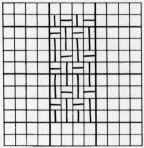

Weft floats **below** the surface would look like this, with the plain weave shown as covering the float entirely (Fig. 2).

Fig. 2

So a weft thread which passes from the front to the back of the cloth would be set down on point-paper as follows:

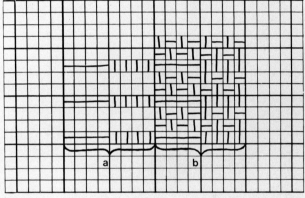

Fig. 3

The first stage (floats only) of setting down such a weave is shown in Fig. 3a. Fig. 3b shows the plain weave ground added.

Often a simple system of warp floats needs only use 3 shafts (2 shafts for the plain weave and 1 for the float end).

When planning floats on point-paper, it is useful to remember that although the float yarn may lie on top or below the plain weave base, without affecting its appearance, it must still be allocated a line on point-paper, with the plain weave continuing on either side of it as though not interrupted. So weft floats on the surface would look like this (Fig. 1).

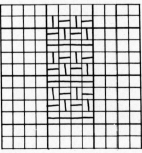

Fig. 1

Alternate coloured ends float alternately on the front and the back of this cloth. Sometimes when they float on the surface they are backed by a coloured weft stripe: the different backing colours affect the apparent colour of the floating ends. (Rhona Whittle, Glasgow School of Art)

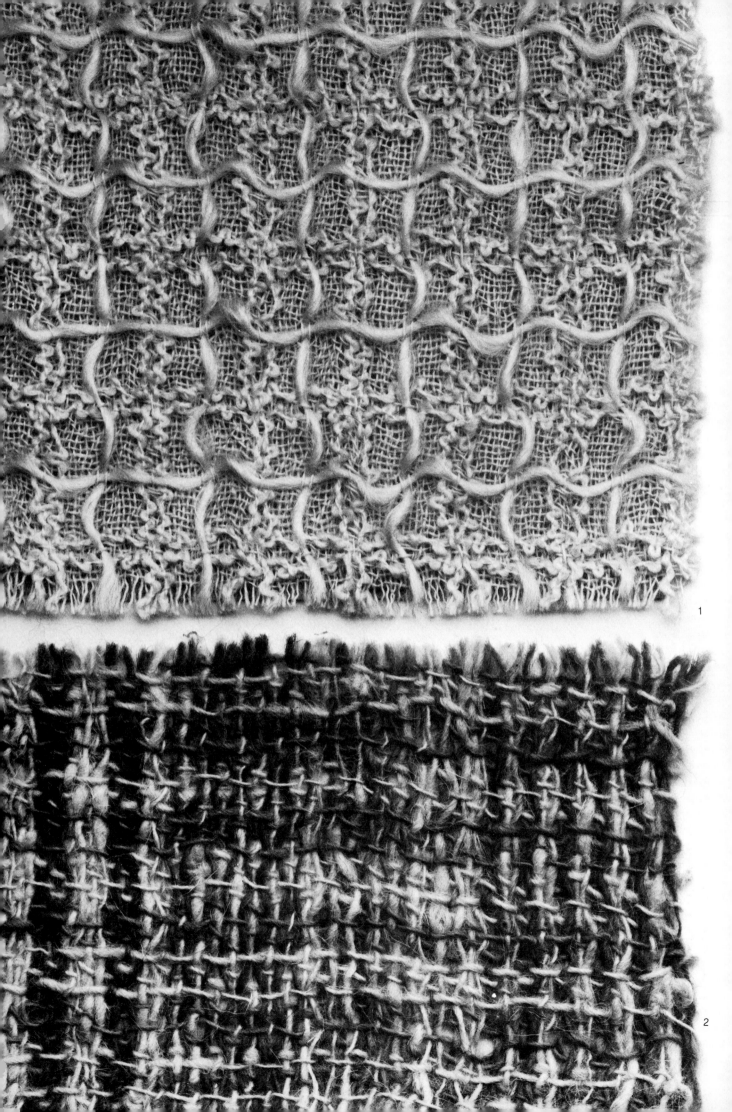

1

2

3

4

Distorted warp and weft floats

When floats occur in both warp and weft, and are arranged to overlap each other so that the floated thread is free to wander aside in one direction only, a distorted illusion results. This distortion does not, of course, show on point-paper.

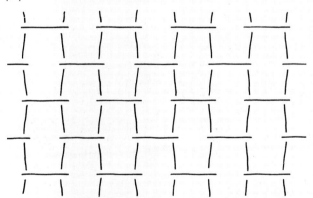

Fig. 1

In Fig. 1 the warp threads are seen to distort: by turning the diagram on its side, weft distortion is explained,

Fig. 2

Fig. 2 is an example of the way this would appear in the point-paper draft. Fig. 3 shows a weave with a longer float.

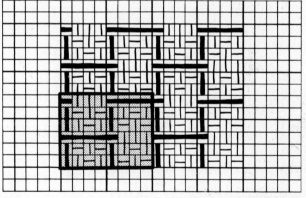

Fig. 3

In both these drafts, for clarity, the floats have been indicated by a thicker line.

1. All mohair fabric in two thicknesses of singles yarn and a gimp. The combination of the character of the thick singles, and the long floats in the weave, produce a marked distortion. (David John Currie)
2. Coarse hand-spun wool woven with distorted threads in the warp. (Pat Holtom)
3. Distorted threads in the warp.
4. Distorted threads in the weft.

2

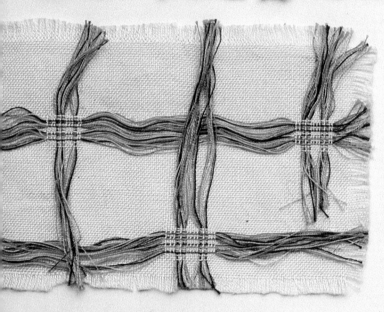

1

3

Clipped Floats

Floats in either warp or weft can, providing they also weave into the base cloth for a distance, be cut to form a short fringe or pile. With a long float, it may be possible to clip away most of the floating thread, leaving a short fringe where the float leaves and enters the base cloth. This trimming is usually done after the cloth has been removed from the loom, especially in the case of warp floats, where the tension could be lost if ends were cut at any point.

The double corduroy rug technique is an example of cut weft floats. The weft to be cut weaves in the base cloth for a while between each float so that the pile will be held firmly in place during use. The floats are staggered so that the pile can be denser.

1 & 2 Groups of coloured threads designed to weave in for part of the cloth only, with long floats designed to be cut away when the cloth is finished. Shown before and after clipping. (Diane Bell, West Surrey College of Art and Design)
3. Floats in warpways 'cords' are cut in areas so that they form a pile. (Diane Lawson, West Surrey College of Art and Design)

The simplest form of 'Monk's Belt', with floats equal in width to the ground areas. This can form a satisfying check, which can then be varied by using, for example, different materials, space-dyed yarns or different colours.

Overleaf:
1. Warp floats in a plain weave ground, with areas of crammed-and-spaced threads on either side. (Jane Kimmitt, Manchester Polytechnic)
2. Warp floats in a plain weave ground. The floats are made up of two of more colours. Silk dress fabric. (Klair Casey, West Surrey College of Art and Design)
3. Thick silk weft floating over and under warp bands of fine silk threads. On the alternate bands where the warp is visible on the right side, it changes colour subtly from band to band. ('Siamese Brocade' hand-woven in Thailand for Jack Lenor Larsen, New York, sample supplied by Homeworks, London)

Monk's Belt

A good example of a weave with floats occuring on both sides of the cloth is known to hand-weavers as Monk's Belt. (It is hardly known at all to weave designers for industry.) Probably of Scandinavian origin, Monk's Belt is one of the simplest forms of overshot design. (See page 140.) The floats are in alternating blocks, and because they do not weave into the base cloth at all it is possible to vary the yarns in thickness and material as well as in colour.

135

1

2

3

Overshots

Sometimes a thread will weave into the base fabric for a short distance, float on the reverse of the cloth, and also on the face of the cloth. When the floats are in the weft this is the basis of the huge family of weaves long known to hand-weavers as 'overshot' patterns. These elaborate designs have been woven for centuries in many parts of world, notably in North America where they have been used extensively in weaving bedcovers. Fascinating to weave but for some time dismissed as unfashionable and 'crafty', overshots can be given a new lease of life by taking advantage of the weft floats of this weave to introduce original and exotic yarns. Such yarns can be shown to advantage by any float, but added to the complexity of the overshot patterning, they can produce rich results.

Weaving overshot patterns in thick yarns, instead of the more usual thin linens and cottons, automatically enlarges the design possibilities without the necessity of changing the weave structure. For all their elaborate appearance, overshot patterns rarely use more than 4 shafts, and to weave one is to realize the many permutations of threading and lifting available on this number of shafts.

It is perfectly possible to design new overshot patterns. To understand the principles involved it is advisable at first to weave a few traditional designs. Then it is possible to start evolving variations on these by leaving out certain areas and expanding others in warp and weft.

Traditional overshaft pattern 'Wandering Vine', or 'Snail Trail'. It is woven here with a warp of several colours, and a chenille yarn forming the overshot pattern. This design is woven on 4 shafts. See page 191 for the draft. (Pat Holtom)

Previous page:
1. Furnishing fabric of weft floats on a worsted ground – the floats are double the width of the ground stripe, and vice versa on the reverse. (Marion Fernside, West Surrey College of Art and Design)
2. Warp floats of Welsh wool on a hand-spun cotton ground. This fabric was woven on a draw-loom. (Woven c. 1937 by Alice Hindson)

Another traditional overshot: 'Bina and Vin', together with an example of the possibilities of extracting a small part of the original design and repeating it. The draft for this design is on page 191.

Overleaf:
A thick worsted warp and a pattern weft of coarse, hand-spun wool enlarge this traditional 'Blooming Leaf' overshot design to dramatic proportions. The draft for this design is on page 191. (Pat Holtom)

1

1. Traditional overshot, 'Maria Collins' No.162', and a version of it which can be obtained by selecting the lifts in a different order.
2. 'Johann Speck's No.33' is a handsome flower motif – another traditional overshot design – woven here with a loop mohair pattern weft. The drafts for these designs are on page 191. (Pat Holtom)

2

Overleaf:
Very long floats are possible when a yarn such as brushed mohair, with its 'clinging' properties, is used. These interlaced areas of floats in a plain weave ground are shown before and after being tied up with coloured wools. (A.S.)

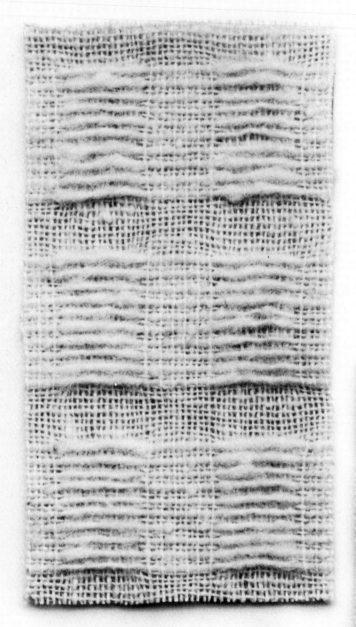

1

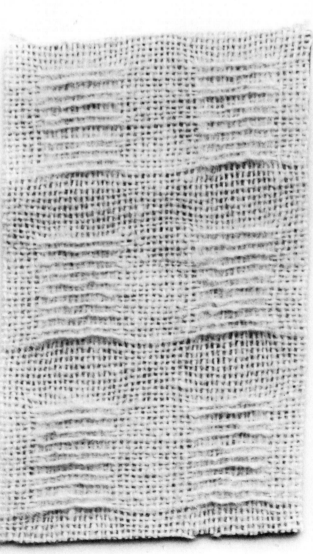

2

3

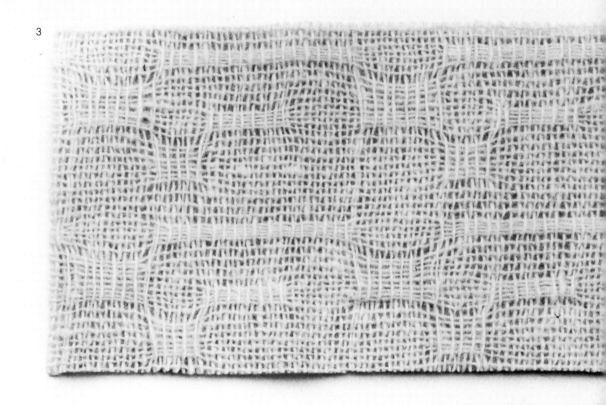

1. & 2. Long floats are again used in these simple woollen curtain fabrics. In 1. the same yarn is used for the floats as for the plain weave ground; in 2. a thicker yarn has been used, making a bolder and heavier cloth. ('Libra' and 'Gemini', designed by Peter Simpson, R.D.I., Bute Fabrics Ltd)

3. Clusterings of weft threads where several work as one in certain areas, causing warp floats of up to ¾ inch in length. These are practical in curtain fabrics because of the felting properties of the woollen yarns used. ('Capricorn', designed by Peter Simpson, R.D.I., Bute Fabrics Ltd)

Mock Lenos

There are many ways of weaving an open, lacy fabric. Several of these ways involve the crossing-over of pairs, or groups, of warp ends so that the picks are held slightly apart, making small holes in the cloth. This can be done manually, on the simplest of looms, or with the help of special 'doup' heddles, as used in industrial weaving. This is called 'gauze' or 'leno' weaving, and involves various combinations of one, or more, warp threads crossing over or under its immediate neighbour (Fig. 1).

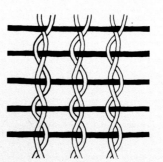

Fig. 1

3-, 4- and 5-end mock lenos are common (Figs. 3, 4, 5 and 6).

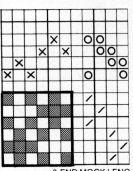

Fig. 3   3-END MOCK LENO

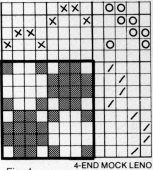

Fig. 4   4-END MOCK LENO

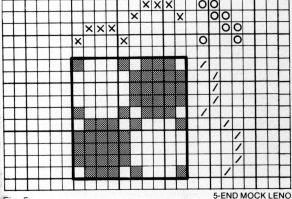

Fig. 5   5-END MOCK LENO

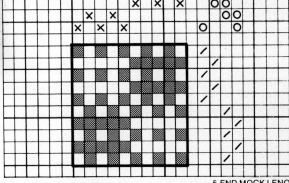

Fig. 6   5-END MOCK LENO

There are, however, ways of producing a lacy cloth by simple weave structure without any special equipment. This group of weaves is called 'imitation gauze', or, more popularly, 'mock leno'. Small groups of warp and/or weft threads are encouraged, by the interlacing, to slide together so that small holes are formed in the fabric. Most 'mock lenos' consist of a warp float motif counter-changed with a weft float motif. This grouping can take place with as few as 3 threads per group (Fig. 2).

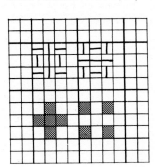

Fig. 2

Warp stripes of plain weave, basket weave and mock leno in a 4-shaft fabric which also includes a variety of yarns and fibres: mercerised cotton, singles cheviot wool and woollen gimp. (Jean Horn, Glasgow School of Art)

The way in which the warp is sleyed in the reed can assist the formation of these groups of threads. By grouping all the threads of one unit in one dent, so that a reed wire lies between the groups, the pattern will be pronounced. If it is possible to leave an empty dent between the groups the lace effect will be even more increased (Fig. 1).

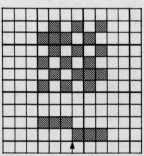

Reed plan: leave empty dent at arrow if possible.

Fig. 1

By examining the drafts it will be seen that some mock lenos can be combined with areas of plain weave in both warp and weft, without involving the use of extra shafts (Figs. 2 and 3). Warp or weft stripes can be planned. Square and rectangular areas of mock leno surrounded by plain weave can also be planned without using more than 4 shafts. If more shafts are available, it is possible to weave simple shapes of mock leno in a plain ground.

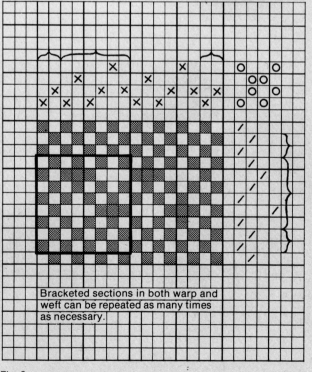

Bracketed sections in both warp and weft can be repeated as many times as necessary.

Fig. 2

154

2

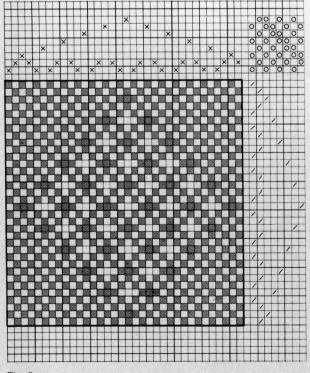

Fig. 3

Where areas of mock leno are surrounded by plain weave, special sleying cannot be used. This would disturb the regularity of the plain weave areas.

1. Mock leno curtain in mohair singles, with gimp used in the weft through the centre of every other group of three picks. (David John Currie)
2. Hand-spun yarns, singles and plied, are used to accentuate the lacy character of this mock leno, designed for a shawl. It was woven on 6 shafts, and has a plain weave border. (Nancy Goschen, West Surrey College of Art and Design)

Mock leno is usually regarded as a texture weave, used for openwork effects. It is often woven in white or pale colours, and is rarely enhanced by the use of colour. However, it is possible to produce a cloth in which the colour is an integral part of the design, by judicious placing of colour to coincide with strategic parts of the weave. Sometimes the weave and yarn alone would not be sufficiently interesting.

1. All-silk dress fabric in 3-end mock leno with a large check in the design formed by a contrast colour placed at the central end pick of each group of three, keeping the background a constant scarlet. (Annabelle Aguire, West Surrey College of Art and Design)
2. Pairs of coloured wool ends and picks outlining thick white wool in a 4-end mock leno. (A.S.)

Overleaf:
1. Areas of mock leno and plain weave in a crisp curtain fabric of natural brown alpaca and camel hair. The mock leno in this case is a curious one – a 3-pick, 4-end mock leno. ('Woodbine', woven in Ireland for Jack Lenor Larsen, New York, sample supplied by Homeworks, London)
2. Rectangles of 3-end mock leno in which the centre end of each unit of three is doubled up (apparent in the plain weave areas above and below the pattern blocks). This is, therefore, also a 3-pick, 4-end mock leno, but needing only 4 shafts. (Maureen Austin, West Surrey College of Art and Design)

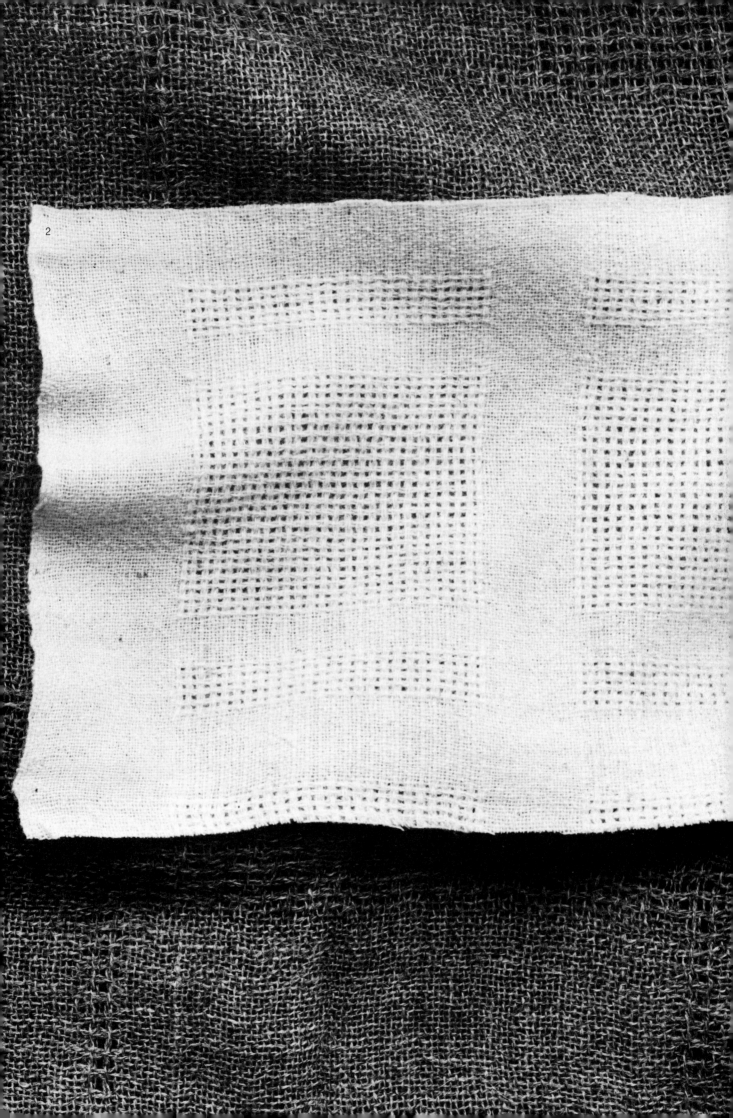

1   2

1. Brighton honeycomb, woven on 8 shafts.
2. 5-shaft honeycomb showing reverse. The coloured threads on
   the ridges of the honeycomb cells on the back of the cloth
   become spots of colour in the depths of the cells on the front.
   (Jane Martin, West Surrey College of Art and Design)

Honeycombs

Warp and weft floats arranged around a small plain weave area form raised squares with sunken centres when the cloth is removed from the loom and the yarns allowed to contract. This cellular structure, aptly called **honeycomb** is not only visually effective, but also provides a high standard of insulation against cold. For this reason it is traditionally used for blankets, where the pockets of air trapped by the weave conserve body heat very efficiently. When woven in cotton or linen yarns, the floats can absorb moisture readily, and the weave can be seen in some hand-towels and tea-towels.

It is usual for both warp and weft to be of the same yarn, and for the cloth to be balanced. As with all weaves, the sett will influence the performance of the fabric. In honeycomb, if the sett is too loose there is a danger of the 'cells' flattening in use, losing to some degree the useful pockets of air.

There are two types of honeycomb: ordinary and Brighton. **Ordinary honeycomb** has the cellular structure on both sides of the cloth – it is usually woven with a point draft and needs a minimum of 4 shafts (Fig. 1).

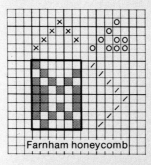

Farnham honeycomb

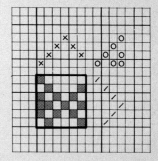

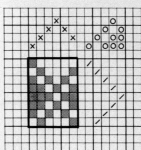

Fig. 1

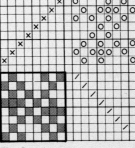

Brighton honeycomb has the honeycomb effect on one side of the cloth only, and is woven on a straight draft. It needs a minimum of 8 shafts (Fig. 2).

Fig. 2

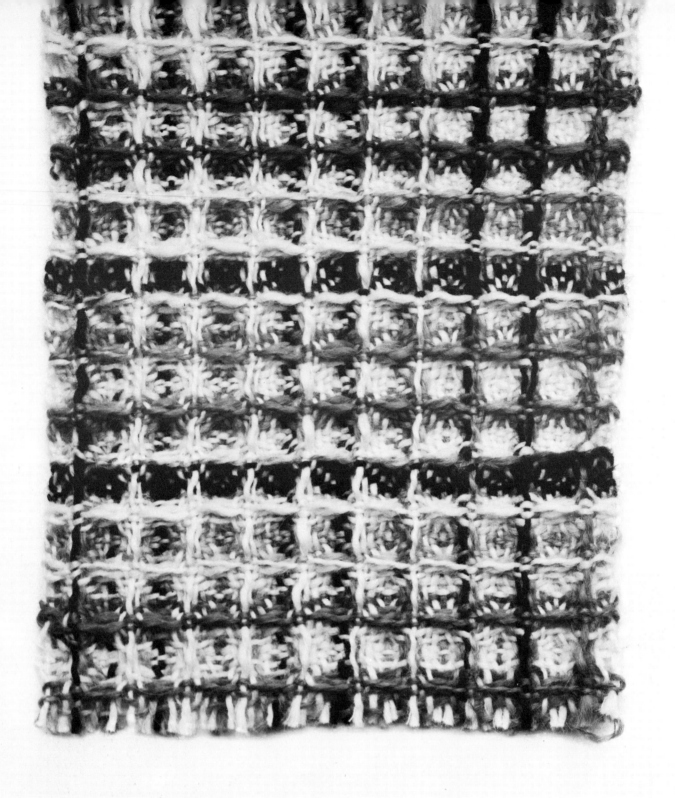

Honeycomb on 5 shafts woven using space-dyed worsted spiral in both warp and weft.

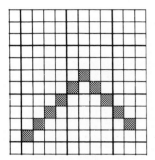

Ordinary honeycombs can be constructed to occupy as many shafts as are available. Taking, as example, 6 shafts, a pointed draft is entered on the point-paper. Vertical marks, or filled-in squares, instead of the crosses used to indicate the order of threading (Fig. 1).

Fig. 1

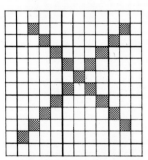

Then the point is inverted for the top half of the draft, until a repeat is reached (Fig. 2).

Fig 2

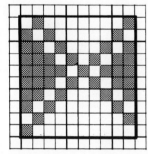

Then opposite pairs of triangular spaces are filled in (Fig. 3).

Fig. 3

Although these drafts appear diagonal on paper, the resulting cloths will have square or rectangular 'cells'. If the structure in Fig. 3 is woven, the weft floats will be longer than the warp floats. This can be reversed, but the warp and weft floats will always be uneven. If they are evened up, then the 'cell' becomes rectangular instead of square (Fig. 4).

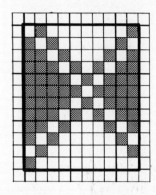

Fig. 4

A straight, rather than a point, draft makes a slightly more satisfactory arrangement possible. The original base marks are staggered in their double V-formation. However, a minimum of 8 shafts is necessary for this draft (Fig. 5).

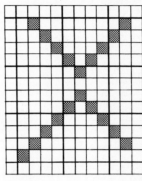
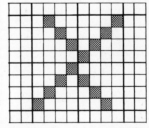
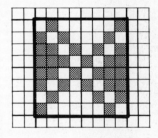

Fig. 5

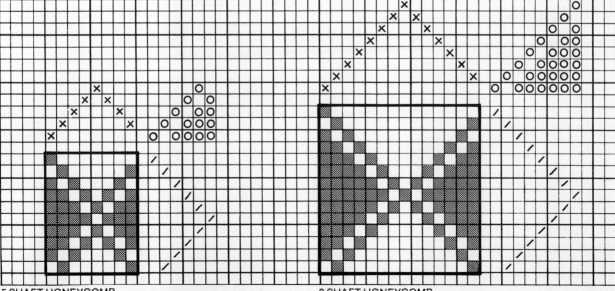

5 SHAFT HONEYCOMB

8 SHAFT HONEYCOMB

2

1. Coloured or textured yarns can be introduced into a honeycomb weave at strategic points for various reasons. This example, woven on 6 shafts, includes several tones of yarn to give the illusion of cutting back through layers. Thick yarns were used to increase the scale, and the depth, of the cell. (Pat Holtom)
2. Commonly available tea-towel in cotton – woven in honeycomb for maximum absorbency.

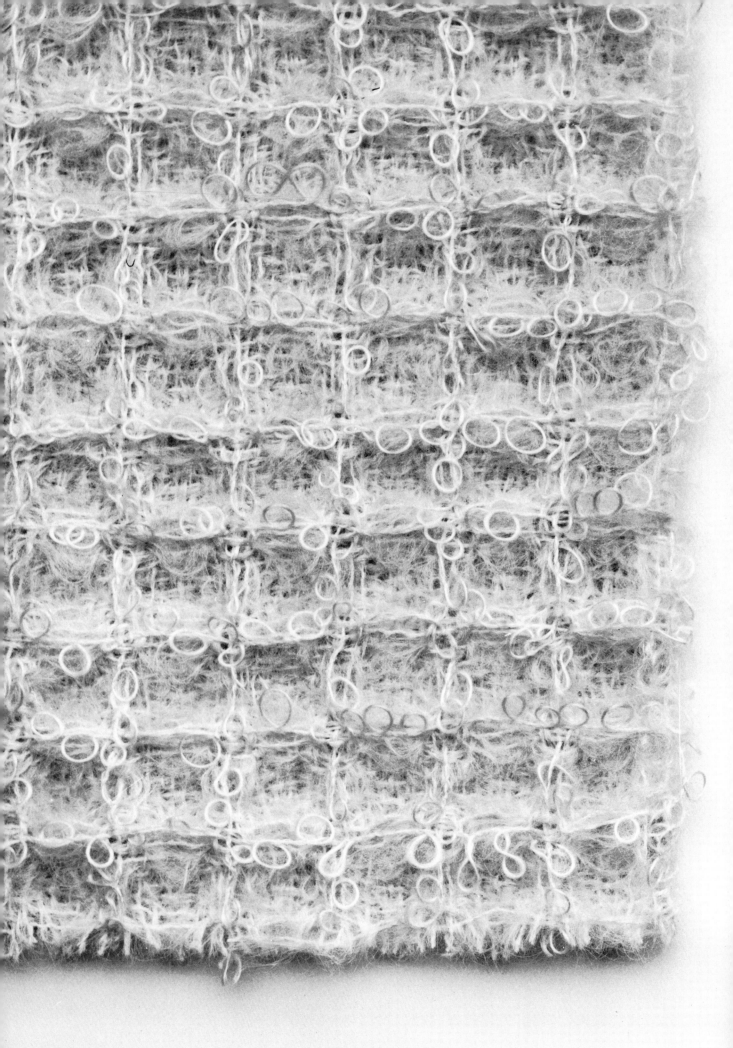

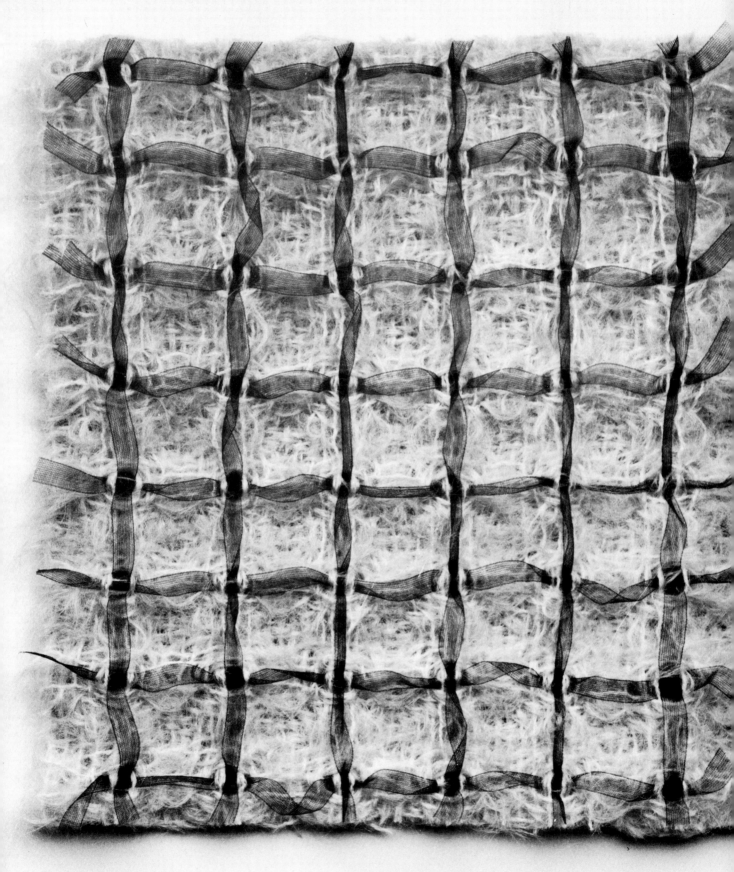

Large-scale honeycombs of brushed mohair (woven on 6 shafts). In one case, the long top threads of the cells are in silk organza ribbon; in the other, large loop mohair. (A.S.)

Cords

A cloth can be constructed so that it has prominent ribs, or cords, on the surface. These can run in the direction of either the warp or the weft. The ribs are usually not more than 1 inch (2.5 cm) wide. Many different widths of cord can be planned in the same cloth. If the loom has a rising shed, corded fabrics are usually woven face down to save lifting the majority of the shafts with each shed formed.

Weftways cords

Cords running across the cloth, from selvedge to selvedge, are sometimes called welts, or even piqués. (However, the word piqué is now more commonly used to describe a lightweight, narrow-rib Bedford cord cloth, see page 170.) The structure is different in several ways from that of the warpways cord. Two warps are used; one for the floats at the back of the cord, kept at a high tension on a separate beam; the other, which remains at a slacker tension, appearing on the surface of the ribs. Padding picks can be inserted, then both top and bottom warps weave together to make the indentation between the ribs. The two warps can both be of the same quality, so that either warp can come to the surface; or the backing warp can be a strong, fine yarn and remain on the back except between ribs.

Weftways cord cloth in wool: the warp is all white, with the colours inserted in the weft, sometimes pick-and-pick. The cords are heavily padded with wool roving. (Catherine Carmichael, Glasgow School of Art)

Warpways cords

When the cords run parallel to the warp, the weave is known as 'Bedford cord'. The rib is formed by pairs of weft threads weaving into the warp ends of the first cord, and floating right under the next. The second pair of picks will float under the first cord and weave into the next one. To provide a firm structure, pairs of ends working in plain weave usually lie between the ribs. However, cords can also be woven without these pairs of plain weave ends. When planning the denting for Bedford cord, the ribs can be accentuated by splitting up the pairs of plain weave ends in the reed, so that they lie in adjacent dents.

A highly twisted yarn as weft will contract in the floats at the back of the cords, pulling them into fuller ribs. A more even roundness can be achieved by incorporating thick, soft padding or wadding threads, which lie between the surface of the rib and the weft floats on the reverse. These wadding ends do not normally appear on the surface. Because they do not weave in, they will not 'take-up' in length, and will need to be beamed, or weighted, separately. It is customary to insert one wadding thread after every two warp threads, rather than one thick thread which might not pass easily through the reed. Their presence should not affect the surface of the cloth, and they should not be calculated in as part of the sett of the surface cloth. They can be made to weave into the floats at the back of the cords for a more hardwearing cloth, but the prominence of the ribs will then be reduced. If needed they can be brought to the surface in places as a decorative spot, but this will also reduce the fullness of the rib.

A standard, unpadded, Bedford cord draft, starts off with the pairs of plain weave, spaced an even number of ends apart (Fig. 1).

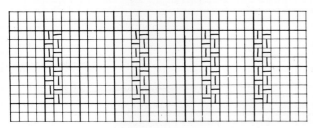

Fig. 1

Then the pairs of picks are inserted, weaving and floating in alternate cords (Fig. 2).

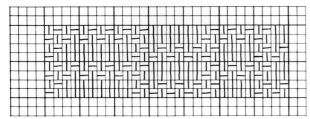

Fig. 2

If wadding threads are to be used they must, of course, be shown on the draft. To avoid confusion, they are shown as dotted lines in Fig. 3.

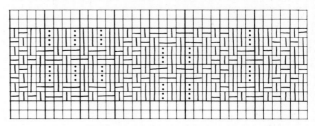

Fig. 3

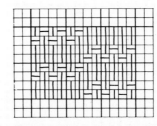

Fig. 4

This padded Bedford cord needs 8 shafts. If the padding were omitted only 6 shafts would be needed, and by leaving out the pairs of plain weave a warp rib can be woven on 4 shafts. (Fig. 4).

A Bedford cord can also be woven with picks weaving singly instead of in pairs in alternate ribs. When drafting this it is necessary either to set the plain weave ends in opposing pairs each time, or to plan the ribs with odd numbers of ends.

1. Bedford cord stripes with several plain weave ends between padded cords. ('Douglas', Placide Joliet, France, sample supplied by Homeworks, London)
2. Flat, unpadded Bedford cord in white wool curtain fabric in which every other pick weaves into a crammed band of ends, while the others pass beneath ('Aquarius 1', designed by Peter Simpson, R.D.I., Bute Fabrics Ltd)
3. Closely woven Bedford cord using S-and Z-twist yarns in order to disturb the surface. (Yvonne Wilkinson, West Surrey College of Art and Design)

171

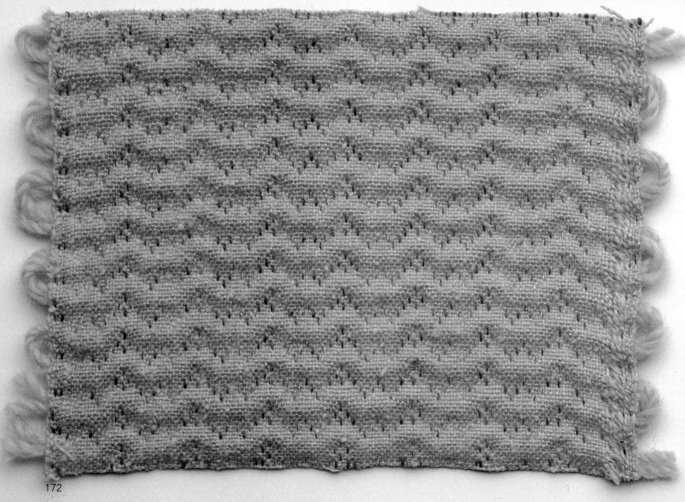

Waved piqués

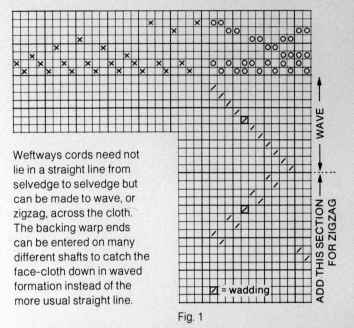

Weftways cords need not lie in a straight line from selvedge to selvedge but can be made to wave, or zigzag, across the cloth. The backing warp ends can be entered on many different shafts to catch the face-cloth down in waved formation instead of the more usual straight line.

☑ = wadding

WAVE

ADD THIS SECTION
FOR ZIGZAG

Fig. 1

The backing warp 'stitches' the face-cloth down in waved or diamond-shaped areas. Then the wadding threads are inserted, and another series of waves or diamonds are woven, positioned in between, or immediately below, the shapes of the first row. Thus the wadding threads are forced into waved lines across the cloth. It is essential that the backing warp is tensioned separately and more tightly than the face-cloth warp.

Waved piqués showing typical wave or diamond shapes made by the tightly-tensioned backing threads. In these cloths the backing threads are of space-dyed cotton, to add extra colour variety in the hollows. The wadding threads are visible at the selvedges. (Pat Holtom)

2   1   3

1. Weftways cord with alternating cords of thick mohair singles, and wool gimp (used alternately with mohair singles). The twist in the singles mohair is solely responsible for the waves in the singles cords. Padded. (David John Currie)
2. A Bedford cord where the surface weave is 2/2 twill, reversing in direction on alternating cords. All wool. Padded. (D.S.437, designed by Peter Simpson, R.D.I., Bute Fabrics Ltd)
3. 4-shaft double cloth in cotton – one side striped, the other side plain; changing sides for one narrow band only. **See overleaf for other side of the same cloth.** (Anna Crutchley, West Surrey College of Art and Design)

See page 175 for reverse of cloth.

Double Cloth

Double, triple and multiple cloths are two or more complete cloth layers woven, one above the other, at the same time. This feat of weaving is done for several reasons: often in order to make a bulkier or stronger cloth, or for warmth. Decorative possibilities occur when adjacent areas of solid colour are available.

Double cloths can be woven:
a. so that they remain separate at both selvedges (in which case they would fall away from one another completely on being taken off the loom);
b. so that they are joined at one selvedge and open down the other (if this is done carefully, cloth which is twice the width of the loom will be the result);
c. so that they are joined together at both selvedges, making a tube of cloth (an uneven number of ends is needed for this).

All these results are controlled by the number and direction of the shuttles.

The two cloths can also be interchanged to practical and decorative effect, so that the two cloths change places from front to back in areas, warpways and/or weftways.

Usually woven in balanced plain weave, each basic cloth needs 2 shafts. So a black cloth on top, and a white one below needs 4 shafts. There are pattern possibilities which do not need more shafts. For example, stripes or colour-and-weave in the warp and/or weft; simple weftways interchange of the two cloths so that white comes to the top and black is below.

If warpways interchange of the cloths is needed, then another 4 shafts will be necessary. So for a chequerboard pattern 8 shafts would be required.

Where the finished cloth will be exposed to friction, the interchanges should be frequent so that one cloth is not able to rub on the other, or to hang away.

Sometimes the possibility of pouching or puckering is decoratively desirable, and it can be encouraged by using two very different yarns for the cloths, one of which is more elastic than the other or which will shrink more than the other in finishing.

If the appearance of two plain cloths, back to back, is wanted, then the odd 'stitching' end can be included in the draft so that one warp end goes through to the other side and back, at intervals of about 1 in (2.5 cm). This should be invisible in the finished cloth.

Once the drafting of double cloths, in which both cloths are in plain weave and at the same sett, is mastered, variations can be tried using two different weaves or very different yarns which need different settings.

Areas of single cloth with pockets of double cloth or double cloth with 'quilting' panels of single cloth are both possible. It must be remembered that the single cloth will be twice as dense as the double cloth areas.

Triple cloth

If each layer of plain weave takes 2 shafts, then three layers, for triple cloth, will take 6 shafts. The three cloths can be

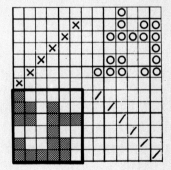

woven in a zigzag way, so that they open out to three times the width of the warp when finished. They can also interchange weftways. (To interchange warpways would take more shafts than are available on most handlooms.)

Drafting a double cloth

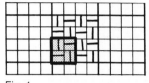

Fig. 1

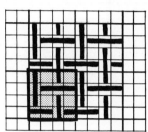

Fig. 2

One of the easiest ways to draft a double cloth is to put down the top cloth on point-paper as a 'blown up' plain weave. So, if plain weave is this (Fig. 1), then the same weave, blown up so that there is one space between each end and pick, would be (Fig. 2).

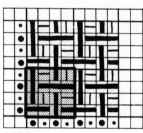

Fig. 3

This is the top layer of cloth. It is a good idea to mark it in with dark lines. The bottom layer of cloth can be filled in the remaining squares, again in 'spaced out' plain weave, in a lighter line (Fig. 3).

Fig. 3 is the weave plan for two separate layers of plain cloth, one over the other. It is easier to understand the interlacing especially when beginning, if the vertical/horizontal mark method of drafting is used.

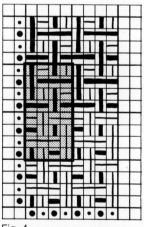

Fig. 4

The next step is to be able to show in the weave plan how one cloth can interchange with another in a weftways direction. To do this, draw an area of Fig. 3, and then, **noting very carefully which threads were the bottom layer on that plan**, draw in another area of double cloth below the first, making these light threads form the top layer of 'blown up' plain weave. Fill in the back layer as before. The lighter lines now form the top cloth, and the darker ones are on the bottom layer (Fig. 4).

4-shaft horizontal striped double cloth; the stripes can be changed in depth without affecting the number of shafts needed. Black stripes are white on the reverse, and vice versa. (A.S.)

When working out the threading and lifting, no account is, of course, taken of 'light' or 'dark' marks only of the combinations of vertical and horizontal marks (Fig. 5).

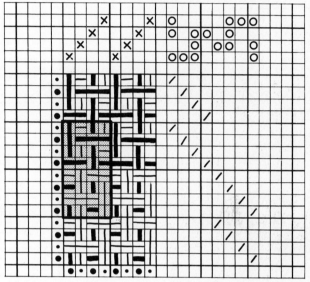

Fig. 5

The same interchange of top and bottom cloths can be made in a warpways direction, and the resulting chequerboard design needs 8 shafts (Fig. 6).

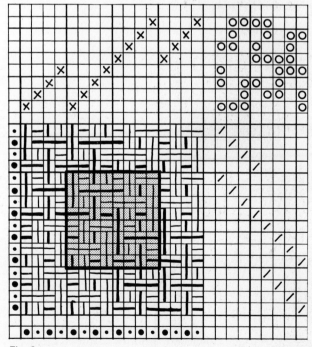

Fig. 6

Although there are, of course, many points at which one weave can be joined on to another, it is wise to keep the dark, light, dark, light, sequence unbroken in both warp and weft.

1

2

1. Subtle use of white silk and white merino wool in double cloth chequerboard needing 8 shafts. (Jennifer Jones, West Surrey College of Art and Design)
2. Upholstery fabric in wool double cloth, chequerboard squares. Perfectly related colour combinations are possible in this technique. (Jessica Cox, West Surrey College of Art and Design)

Overleaf:
The combination of double cloth areas with plain weave produces rounded forms, where all the threads from both layers of cloth pack into one layer. This also gives a hairline stripe, reversing direction on the other side. Both sides of the cloth (a blanket) are shown. (Jessica Cox, West Surrey College of Art and Design)

See pages 184/185
Double cloth squares in linen, with a colour change partway across each square. Before the shed was changed to seal off a square and start another, a sheet of coloured acetate was slipped inside. (Pat Holtom)

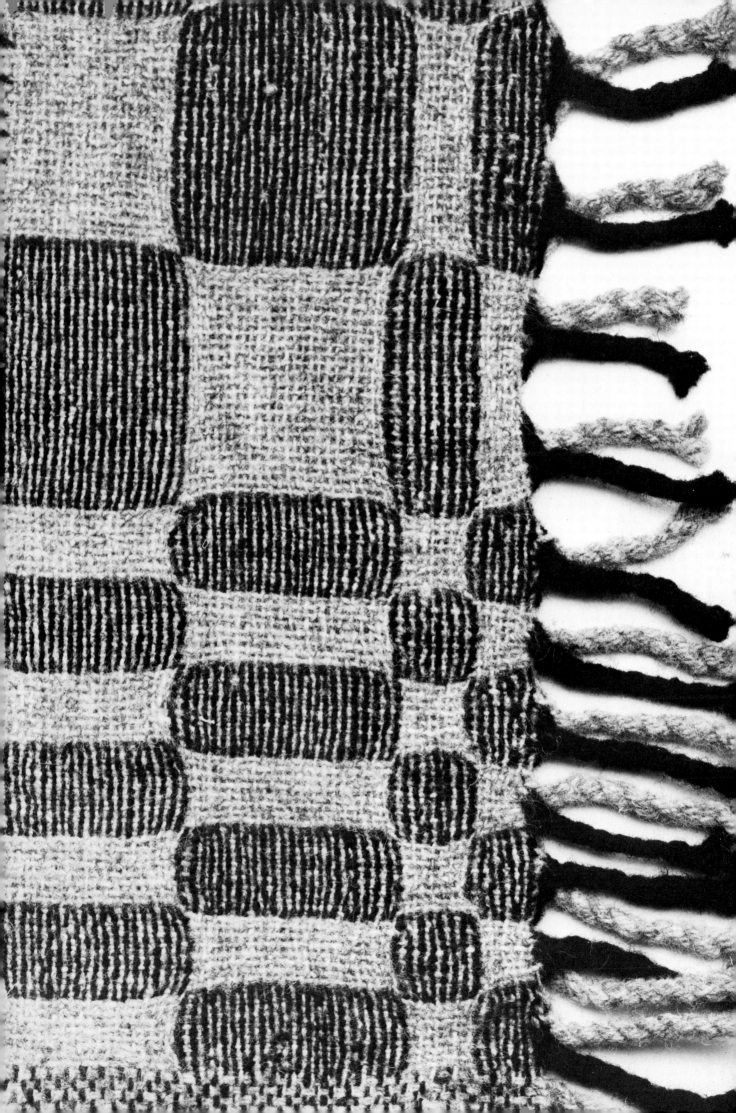

2a

2b

1. Double cloth combined with ikat. Cotton. (Sarah Sumsion, Glasgow School of Art)
2. Two double cloths designed to be used together. (a) Changes of layer appear to be in both directions but this is caused by the weft colour change, and the weave reverses in warpways stripes only. (b) Two plain cloths woven at once and joined throughout by single ends at intervals of 1½ inches. (Eva Pettigrew, West Surrey College of Art and Design)

1. Worsted double cloth showing possible colour permutations. Six colours of yarn are used on a black ground. (Allison Blair, Glasgow School of Art)
2. Simple chequerboard double cloth with several colours used together in the warp in one example. Two variations. (A.S.)
3. Double cloth pockets, surrounded by plain weave and twill, containing scraps of coloured fibres. (Cathie Leaver, Loughborough College of Art)

Glossary

BALANCED	See 'Balance and Sett' section (pages 8–11). Sometimes also used to describe an 'even' twill, e.g. 2/2 twill.
DENT	The space between two wires in a reed.
END-AND-END	Sequence of alternating ends of two different colours/yarns.
ENDS	Warp threads.
EPI	Ends per inch (metric counting is usually over 10cm).
ENTERING	Threading the warp ends through the heddles.
FELL	The point during the process of weaving where the last pick has been placed.
FLOAT	Any warp or weft thread passing over three or more threads on back or front of cloth.
LIFTING	Raising shafts by any method.
OVERSHOT	A term applied to a group of traditional weaves on 4 shafts, where alternate picks float on the surface in elaborate patterning.
PICK-AND-PICK	Sequence of alternating picks of two different colours/yarns.
PICKS	Weft threads.
PPI	Picks per inch (metric counting is usually over 10cm).
POINT DRAFT	Entering in consecutive order and reversing, i.e. 1, 2, 3, 4, 3, 2, etc.
POINT-PAPER	Squared paper designed for working out weaves; similar to graph paper.
PLY, PLIED	Twisting two or more singles yarns together.
SETT, SET	See 'Balance and Sett' section, pages 8–11.
SINGLES	A thread of fibres twisted together but not plied.
SKELETON TIE	Each pedal on the loom is tied, via a lam, to one shaft only. Several pedals can be depressed at one time for different combinations of lift. It is popularly used when designing on the loom, for freedom of decision.
SLEYING	Threading the warp ends through the reed.
STRAIGHT DRAFT	Entering in consecutive order and repeating, i.e. 1, 2, 3, 4, 1, 2, 3, 4, etc.
TEXTILE	A woven cloth.
WARP UP	A point where a warp thread lies on the surface.

Booklist

Albers, Anni, **On Weaving** (Wesleyan U.P., 1965; Studio Vista, 1966; paperback 1974). Intellectual approach to structure. Full of common sense and good illustrations.

Ashenhurst, T. R., **Design in Textile Fabrics** (Cassell & Co). 100-year-old book on structure. Out of print, but worth looking out for.

Collingwood, Peter, **The Techniques of Rug Weaving** (Faber, 1968). The definitive book on the subject, and essential for any rug-weaver. Primarily structure.

Davison, Marguerite P., **A Handweaver's Pattern Book** (privately published by the author, 19th edition USA 1977). The most comprehensive collection of traditional overshot patterns: photos and drafts, set out clearly.

Emery, Irene, **The Primary Structures of Fabrics** (The Textile Museum, Washington, USA). Excellent erudite tome of brilliantly classified structures, used by museums, archaeologists, etc. as well as weavers.

Kirby, Mary, **Designing on the Loom** (Studio Vista; Select Books, paperback, 1973). Comprehensive book on structure with nostalgic 1950s examples. Much used in colleges.

Oelsner, G. H., **A Handbook of Weaves** (Dover Publications, new edition 1975). Unaltered reprint of seventy-year-old book of weaves for industry. A curiosity, useful for the experienced weaver.

Straub, Marianne, **Hand Weaving and Cloth Design** (Pelham Books, 1977). Good practical book of which half is on structure. Excellent chapter on double- and multi-layer cloths.

Sutton, Ann, Collingwood, Peter and St Aubyn Hubbard, Geraldine, **The Craft of the Weaver** (BBC Publications, 1981). An attempt to present the basics of the many aspects of the craft of weaving in a clear and sound way. Ideal for beginners.

The Textile Institute, **Textile Terms and Definitions** (7th edition 1975). Simple and short definitions of most industrial textile terms, including magnified close-ups of weaves.

Watson, William, **Textile Design and Colour** (Butterworth, 7th revised edition Z. Grosicki, 1975). The definitive work on weave structure, popular with students and designers for industry. Excellent, but could be dry and difficult for beginners.

Watson, William, **Advanced Textile Design** (Butterworth, 4th revised edition Z. Grosicki, 1977). The advanced companion to the above volume, included here because it has excellent information on double- and multi-layer cloths.

'Blooming Leaf'

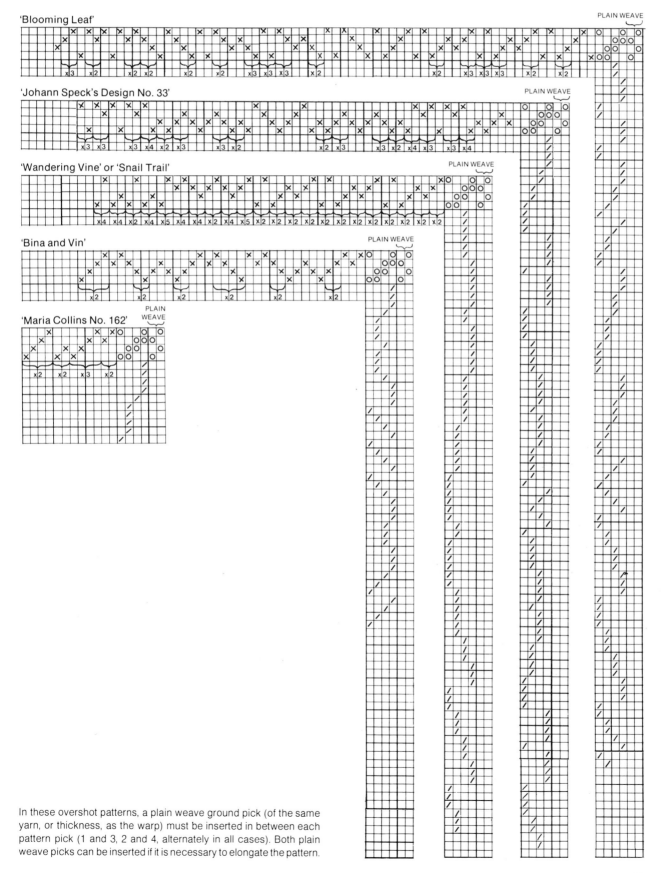

'Johann Speck's Design No. 33'

'Wandering Vine' or 'Snail Trail'

'Bina and Vin'

'Maria Collins No. 162'

In these overshot patterns, a plain weave ground pick (of the same yarn, or thickness, as the warp) must be inserted in between each pattern pick (1 and 3, 2 and 4, alternately in all cases). Both plain weave picks can be inserted if it is necessary to elongate the pattern.

191

Index